THE POWER OF EMPOWERMENT: What the Experts Say
and 16 Actionable Case Studies

"This book is just what serious managers interested in true empowerment need. It's built on a foundation of hard-won learnings and lessons from some of the best, enhanced by the perspective and experience Bill and his experts bring to the subject."
— Carla O'Dell, President, American Productivity & Quality Center

"Full of excellent examples; tells how organizations can make empowerment pay off for them."
— Edward E. Lawler III, Professor of Management and Organization and Director of the Center for Effective Organizations, University of Southern California; author of *From the Ground Up: Six Principles for Building the New Logic Corporation*

"This is an empowerment book that's especially helpful to line managers—whether in manufacturing, services or government. It speaks to their need for principles and examples on how to make it happen."
— Mark Loscudo, Plant Manager, Wilson Sporting Goods Co.

"I think we learn best from stories. Bill Ginnodo has come up with some excellent, real-life empowerment stories."
— William C. Byham, Ph.D., Author of *Zapp! The Lightning of Empowerment* and President/CEO of Development Dimensions International

"It's a book you can get your teeth into. It's loaded with practical advice and great case studies."
— Grace B. Reed, Director, Quality & Business Process Effectiveness, Pratt & Whitney

THE POWER OF EMPOWERMENT

WHAT THE EXPERTS SAY
AND
16 ACTIONABLE CASE STUDIES

RESEARCHED AND EDITED BY
BILL GINNODO

ARLINGTON HEIGHTS, ILLINOIS

The Power of Empowerment. © 1997 by Pride Publications, Inc., 1512 E. Wing St., Arlington Heights, IL 60004.

All rights reserved. No part of this book may be reproduced, stored in a retrieval system, or transmitted, in any form or by any means, electronic or mechanical, including photocopying, recording, or otherwise, except as may be expressly permitted by the United States Copyright Act of 1976 or by prior written permission of the publisher.

The chapter, Empowerment Boundaries at Saturn, included in Part Six, is © 1996 Saturn Corporation, Used With Permission. The Employee Involvement & Empowerment Continuum, Figure 1, included in Part Two, is © 1994 Associates in Continuous Improvement, Inc.

> Substantial discounts on bulk quantities of this book are available to corporations, professional associations, colleges and universities and other organizations. For details and discount information, contact Pride Publications, Inc.: telephone 847-398-0430; fax 847-398-0670; e-mail ginnodo@pridepublications.com

Cover Design: John Berg/LightCraft Graphics, Inc.
Typography: Audrey Spears
Printed in the United States of America by McNaughton & Gunn, Inc.

The paper used in this publication is acid-free and chlorine-free. It meets the requirements of the American National Standard for Permanence of Paper for Printed Library Materials, ANSI Z39.48-1984.

Publisher's Cataloging in Publication *(Prepared by Quality Books Inc.)*
Ginnodo, Bill.
    The power of empowerment : what the experts say and 16 actionable case studies / researched and edited by Bill Ginnodo.
    p.cm.
    Includes bibliographical references and index.
    ISBN 0-9656587-0-8
    1. Employee empowerment—Case studies. 2. Organizational effectiveness. 3. Personnel management. I. Title.

HD50.5.G56 1997   658.3'14
                                              QB197-40102

Library of Congress Catalog Card Number: 97-65436

First Edition/First Printing

CONTENTS

Part One

THE WHO, WHAT, WHEN, WHERE, WHY AND HOW OF EMPOWERMENT

1. What Is It and Why Is It Happening? Why Are Managers Doing It? I'm Still Skeptical, Convince Me. What's My Role and What's In It For Me? 12 Empowerment Principles: How to Make It Work
   Bill Ginnodo 2

Part Two

UNDERSTANDING EMPOWERMENT—WHAT THE EXPERTS SAY

2. Empowerment: There's More to It Than Meets the Eye
   Susan Albers Mohrman, Ph.D. 15
3. Characteristics of an Empowered Organization
   William C. Byham, Ph.D. 24
4. Defining the Boundaries of Empowerment
   Ken Somers, Ph.D. 32
5. Empowerment Roles and Behaviors
   300+ Empowerment Conference Attendees. 44
6. Preparing Supervisors and Employees for Empowerment
   John R. Dew, Ed.D. 51
7. Empowering for Strategic Change: 5 Fundamentals
   Steven A. Leth, Ph.D. 61
8. Determining Your Employee Involvement and Empowerment Strategy
   John N. Younker, Ph.D. 70

Part Three

DEPLOYING AND MANAGING EMPOWERMENT—6 Case Studies

9. Managing Empowerment at Marriott. 79
10. Training for Empowerment at Martin Marietta Energy Systems 90

11	Communicating Empowerment at Federal Express	102
12	Empowerment at Zytec: Letting Go and Taking Charge	113
13	The Plant Manager as Change Agent at Monsanto Chemical	124
14	A Leader's Tool Kit for Transformation at Allstate	135

Part Four

EMPOWERING EMPLOYEES TO SATISFY CUSTOMERS, SOLVE PROBLEMS AND IMPROVE PROCESSES—6 Case Studies

15	Empowerment Through Technology at USAA	149
16	Winning the War on Cycle Time at Motorola	158
17	Reducing Turnaround Time at Swedish American Hospital *Debra G. French and Katherine L. Hermansen*	168
18	Action Forums Save Big Money, Speed Change at PG&E	179
19	Chrysler's Continuous Improvement Workshop Process	190
20	Managing Through Teams at AT&T Microelectronics	201

Part Five

**SELF-DIRECTED TEAMS: THE ULTIMATE IN EMPOWERMENT—
4 Case Studies**

21	Empowerment Boundaries at Saturn *Saturn Corporation*	213
22	Managing the Change to Self-directed Work Teams at Harris Semiconductor	218
23	At AAL, Teams Continue to Pay Off After Seven Years	231
24	Vision, Customer Focus and Teams: Recipe for Success at Tennalum	242

Appendix 1: Management Style—A Quick Self-Assessment ... 255
Appendix 2: Books on Empowerment ... 258
Index ... 261

Dedication

This book is dedicated to those leaders, managers and supervisors in business, industry and government who have learned that sharing power with employees leads not to weakness or anarchy but to stronger, more effective people and organizations.

Acknowledgements

We're especially grateful to the individuals who consented to be interviewed for the case studies in this book, and to the authors who were willing to share their empowerment expertise.

We're also indebted to Frances J. Anderson, Anderson Communications, Inc., for writing many of the case studies.

Part One

The Who, What, When, Where, Why, and How of Empowerment

"If you always do what you've always done, you'll always get what you always got."
—Anonymous

1

The Who, What, When, Where, Why and How Of Empowerment

by Bill Ginnodo

Because I know you're anxious to get to the case studies and the insights of the experts, I've made this introduction short and to the point—and very useful to you.

During the past 11 years, I've been inside 120 organizations, preparing that number of case studies for *Commitment-Plus*, a newsletter which I initially self-published then edited for the Quality & Productivity Management Association (QPMA) and the American Productivity & Quality Center (APQC). Because the newsletter is "For leaders and managers who want to improve productivity, quality and service through people," all of those case studies contained some element of employee involvement or empowerment. Some of them focused entirely on empowerment.

Commitment-Plus subscribers have often suggested that I compile the best of the empowerment case studies in a book that can be shared with a broader audience. They said that the learnings and guiding principles in the stories are timeless and powerful, and that people need to see how those learnings and principles have been put into practice—which should help them both understand and implement empowerment.

I've also been editor of another publication called *Tapping the Network Journal*, published by QPMA, which contained some excellent articles on empowerment. They were written by empowerment experts—consultants who have carefully studied the practice, and practitioners who have participated in its implementation. I've included those articles because each has an important message and contributes to a complete understanding of empowerment.

Each of the articles has been updated by the experts immediately prior to publication of this book. And to ensure that you know what has transpired since the case studies were published, you'll find an epilogue at the end of each of them. That's particularly valuable, because you'll learn that even though some of the organizations have subsequently gone through wrenching change, the empowerment effort survives and has even helped facilitate change.

What Is It and Why Is It Happening?

But before we get to the experts and case studies, you need to know several things, including the definition of empowerment that this book is based upon. It emerged from the several hundred interviews that I conducted for those 120 case studies. It's best understood when compared with traditional management and involvement:

Traditional Management — Managers solve most of the problems and make most of the decisions.

Involvement — Employees have the opportunity to help solve problems and influence decisions.

Empowerment — Employees and managers solve problems and make decisions that were traditionally reserved to higher levels of the organization.

The evolutionary shift from traditional management (command-and-control) to involvement occurred in many organizations in the United States during the 1980's when it became obvious 1) that quality had to be improved if customers' expectations were to be met, and 2) that employees, not just managers, had useful ideas for solving quality problems. Involvement took the form of quality circles, corrective action teams, individual job enrichment, and evolution to a participative style of management.

Beginning in the late 80's and continuing in the 90's, empowerment has been catching on because: management is being pressed by

Baby Boomers and younger people who want more involvement in decision making and more autonomy in their work; employees have shown themselves to be capable of decision making when they're involved; innovative and risk-taking managers have shown that empowerment can work if it's handled correctly; and organizations that have pursued Total Quality Management have shown that empowerment can result in significant improvements in cost, productivity, quality and customer satisfaction. This quality evolution is depicted graphically in Figure 1.

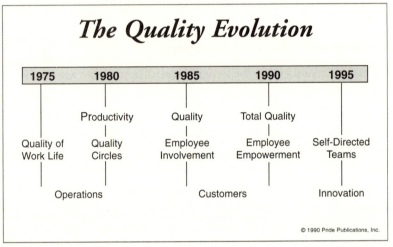

Figure 1

Many organizations in most industries are earning reputations for being part of this evolution and for increasingly empowering their people, including those whose case studies are contained in this book: Aid Association for Lutherans, Allstate, AT&T Microelectronics, Chrysler, Federal Express, Harris Semiconductor, Marriott, Martin Marietta Energy Systems, Monsanto Chemical, Motorola, PG&E, Saturn, Swedish American Hospital, Tennalum, United Services Automobile Association, and Zytec.

As you'll see more clearly when we get to the case studies, empowerment comes in three primary forms:

Individual Empowerment — Individual employees are given authority along with responsibility.

Team Empowerment — Ad hoc teams are formed to solve problems, improve processes or take on a challenge.

Self-Directed Work Teams — Employees are reorganized into teams and have facilitators/coaches instead of supervisors/bosses.

Put simply, *empowerment is giving others the power to take action.* It is not anarchy or abandonment of management's responsibility for effectiveness and results. Whether they work individually or in teams, empowered people feel a strong sense of responsibility for their work and its outcomes, and have greater job satisfaction than those who are not empowered. Good outcomes and increased job satisfaction lead to even more improvement—and the upward spiral continues. Therefore, managers who empower others do not lose power to get things done; they enhance it.

Why Are Managers Doing It?

Whether it's individuals, ad hoc teams or self-directed teams that are empowered, very few of them get there on their own. Some executive, manager or supervisor needs to make it happen. Usually, it's someone whose personal values lean strongly toward collaboration, or someone who becomes convinced of the wisdom of doing it—through observing it in action elsewhere, or by accepting a rationale that makes sense.

Here are the values or beliefs that underlay collaboration with individuals and teams. Along with the definition of empowerment, I gleaned them from the several hundred managers and executives whom I interviewed in the 120 organizations during the past 11 years...

...The Golden Rule applies inside the workplace, too.

...Everyone wants to be treated as an adult.

...We all want to be consulted before decisions are made that affect us.

...People are usually smarter and more capable than we assume they are.

...I don't know everything; collectively, employees will have many more good ideas than I will.

...Nearly everyone wants to do an outstanding job and to be proud of his or her work.

...Commitment to positive outcomes is facilitated by getting barriers out of the way.

...Trust strengthens relationships and performance; distrust weakens them.

...It's up to management to take the first step and lead the way.

Often, managers who initially do not share those values or beliefs become convinced that they should begin empowering people after reading success stories or visiting organizations where empowerment is paying off. Such stories and visits help them visualize it working where they are. For example, they might learn from reading the case studies in this book that...

...Marriott employees have empowerment boundaries that have resulted in improved customer satisfaction and market share.

...A team of employees at Swedish American Hospital reduced average turnaround time of arterial blood gas diagnostic testing for intensive and coronary care patients from 51 minutes to 15.

...Service representatives at USAA have the authority to approve homeowner's insurance up to $300,000.

...Action forums at Pacific Gas & Electric saved the company $300 million over a three and one-half year period.

...In a five-day workshop, employees at Chrysler's Sterling Heights Assembly plant improved walk time 88%, lead time 87%, work-in-process 83% and square-foot utilization 40%.

I'm Still Skeptical; Convince Me

However, beliefs, examples and dramatic improvements sometimes aren't persuasive enough and a provocative dialogue with a superior, colleague, consultant or workshop facilitator is needed to convince managers that empowerment is the way to go. There are usually two fears at work in the minds of resistant managers or supervisors: letting go (Won't the inmates take over the asylum?) and losing power (I don't want to give up control; I want to continue doing things my way). To be successful, the dialogue should help managers understand that their current mind-set is faulted. In a group setting, it might go something like this:

Ask any group of executives, managers or supervisors to define management and they'll readily respond: "Getting work done through people." Then ask them what the primary tasks of management are and they'll say: "To plan, organize, direct and control." Somehow—through education, word-of-mouth, or modeling others' behaviors—most people have come to accept that this is what management is all about.

But ask the same people if there is anything wrong with the Plan-Organize-Direct-Control approach, and they'll just as readily tell you that it leads to...

...underutilization of employees and their ideas—because managers are expected to solve the problems

...preference for the status quo, instead of improvement—because managers already have plates full of operational priorities and crises

...ignoring of customers' real needs—because the focus is on internal operations, and there is little time to interact with customers, and

...organizational performance and results far below what they could be—because employees are underutilized, there's little emphasis on improvement and customers' needs are ignored.

Then ask them to turn that line of thought around and they come up with an interesting conclusion...

...Our performance and results are not what they should or could be.

...We can get better results if we do a better job of satisfying customers.

...To do that, we need to improve.

...And, to improve, we need to use the minds, as well as the hands, of our employees.

The conclusion? Therefore: the Plan-Organize-Direct-Control approach to management is faulted and needs an overhaul; we need a new way to think about the primary tasks (the mind-set) of management. Not that we need to throw away the generic activities of planning, organizing, directing and controlling; they're vital to successful management, and are often delegated to ad hoc and self-directed work teams.

Most of the executives and managers whom I interviewed in those 120 organizations had a very different view of the primary tasks of management. I routinely asked them, "What are you doing differently that's helping your organization with its current success?" Here's what they, collectively, told me:

They're *leading,* which involves articulating a vision, values, strategies and goals; aligning policies, practices and business plans; improving processes; organizing, communicating and "walking the talk" of total quality.

They're *empowering,* by routinely delegating authority to individuals along with responsibility; routinely using corrective, cross-functional, process improvement and self-directed teams; devoting resources to education and training; recognizing and rewarding improvement efforts and success; consulting and coaching employees; and removing barriers that prevent outstanding performance.

They're *assessing,* which involves surveying customer and employee opinions; using quality, productivity and service measures; statistically measuring production processes; and benchmarking the best organizations.

And they're *partnering,* which involves closing the performance gap by working with customers, suppliers, unions and schools; and working with governments and community groups to anticipate and resolve environmental and other issues.

In other words, when an organization focuses on improvement, the primary tasks of management change. My interviewees' experiences with Total Quality Management led them to shift from the traditional Plan-Organize-Direct-Control mind-set to a Lead-Empower-

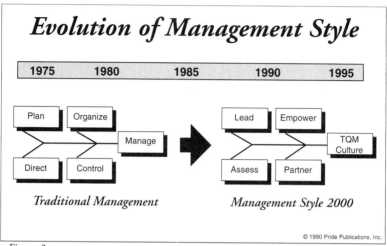

Figure 2

Assess-Partner approach to managing. (The acronym, LEAP, may help you remember this new management style; those who use it seem to LEAP ahead in their quest for better organizational performance.) See Figure 2 for what this shift looks like graphically.

If you refer back to Figure 1, you'll notice that this evolution of management style is consistent with what's been happening in the quality movement during the past 20 years. And it's still evolving—even in the organizations which have strong reputations for empowerment.

By the way, there's an assessment tool in Appendix 1 that may help you determine how far your organization has evolved toward the LEAP mind-set.

What's My Role and What's In It for Me?

But all this management style "stuff" may be too academic or macro for the person who's just beginning to think about empowerment. That individual might have several simple, straightforward questions such as, "What would I do differently? What would the organization get out of it? And what's in it for me?"

The answer to the first question depends upon what the individ-

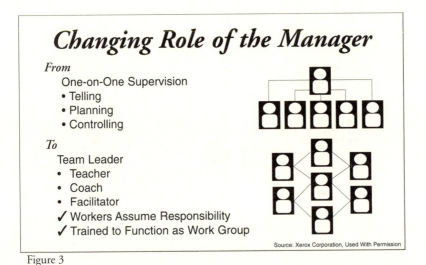

Figure 3

ual's position is within the organization. If he or she is in management, the graphic shown in Figure 3 may provide a good general answer—as it did for Xerox managers.

But, of course, the answer to the role question is more complicated than that, because "management" is made up of people at the executive, middle management and supervisor levels, each of which has its separate demands and expectations. So as to not get unduly bogged down in this question at this point in our discourse, I'd like to suggest that you turn later to the chapter in Section Two titled "Empowerment Roles and Behaviors." For each of five levels in the organization—executives, middle managers, supervisors, employees and the union leadership—the chapter contains a role statement as well as lists of desirable behaviors and behaviors to avoid. The roles and behaviors are the result of intense brainstorming during a national quality conference which focused entirely on empowerment.

As for the question, "What would the organization get out of it?" here is a list of benefits that have also come from my interviews with managers in those 120 organizations...

...Improve the bottom line/competitiveness/market share/fiscal health

...Improve quality/service/customer satisfaction
...Improve productivity/efficiency/throughput/operations/processes/schedules
...Cut cycle time/down-time/setup times
...Reduce costs/errors/rejects/rework/repair/scrap
...Do more with the same number of people
...Develop/invest-in/unleash the potential of the organization's number one resource: people
...Improve employee morale/job satisfaction/commitment/self-motivation/loyalty
...Improve communications/trust/teamwork
...Reduce turnover/absenteeism/grievances/employee unrest
...Improve labor-management/union relations
...Make it easier to introduce changes/use new technology/take risks/adapt to future changes
...Strengthen decision-making and management of the organization
...Reach higher business goals/ensure a brighter future.

Similarly, here is the list of benefits gleaned from my interviewees in response to the question, "What are *you* getting out of it?"...
...More power/accomplishment through people
...Satisfaction of improved organizational performance/situation/turnaround
...More respect/status/recognition/look better
...Less stress/fewer crises
...More time to plan/organize/work on strategic issues
...Satisfaction of seeing people turn on/grow/accomplish something meaningful
...More enjoyment in the day's work
...Empowerment is consistent with personal values
...Become a more effective manager and leader.

12 Empowerment Principles: How to Make It Work

With that stage-setting, we're about ready to dive into the experts' articles and case studies. But, first, we need to look at the guiding principles that I promised earlier. Having them will be like having a special pair of eyeglasses that will help you see the content of the articles and case studies more clearly. To use another metaphor, they can also be your flashlight as you try to find your way through the dark.

The following 12 guiding principles were gleaned from those several hundred people interviewed in 120 organizations over an 11-year period—along with the definition of empowerment, the values which underlay the practice, the LEAP style of management, the empowerment roles and behaviors and the benefits to the organization and its managers. And they're reinforced by what the experts say.

1. There is *no magic formula or standard recipe* for empowerment; each implementation is unique to its situation.

2. Empowerment serves a *purpose*. It's not a feel-good program. It's about accomplishing business objectives. It's a means to an end, not an end in itself. Empowerment helps employees help the organization and themselves; it gives them more meaningful jobs and a sense of accomplishment and pride.

3. Empowerment needs to be *managed*—to make it happen and to make sure it's happening.

4. Empowerment works best when it's *values-based*. More energy is generated when employees believe in their managers and The Cause than when they feel they're just filling a position or marking time.

5. *Trust* and *commitment* are paramount; winning employees' hearts and minds leads to their willing contribution of ideas, loyalty, determination and extra effort.

6. *Managers* and *supervisors* need to be empowered, too.

7. Setting clear *boundaries* tells people what they're authorized to do; removing *barriers* makes it possible for them to do it.

8. *Communication* and *information* are the lifeblood of empowerment.

9. Empowerment *training* is more than remedial; it prepares people for collaboration and higher level performance, and sends a message to employees: we're spending money on you because this is important to the organization's future.

10. *Facilitating* and *coaching* are more effective than directing and controlling—when you want people to grow and contribute.

11. *Celebration* and *recognition* for forward motion and accomplishment are needed, to express genuine thanks and to reinforce the kind of behavior that's wanted.

12. Empowerment is *hard work* and *takes time.* Beliefs, practices, policies, organizational structures and behaviors aren't easily changed.

Now, you're in for a real treat and an enriching experience. I've learned a lot about empowerment from these people whose words, ideas and experiences you'll be reading. I believe you will, too.

Bill Ginnodo's experience with empowerment has come primarily from three sources: study, observation and personal application. Especially during the past 16 years, he has studied what the leading organizations have done to engage their people in productivity and quality improvement efforts, he has interviewed several hundred managers in many of those organizations to observe first hand how they went about involving and empowering their people, and, as a manager himself, he has applied what he's learned from that study and observation.

Bill is currently Publisher of Pride Publications and was previously Executive Director of the Quality & Productivity Management Association (QPMA), Associate Director of the American Productivity & Quality Center (APQC), Productivity and Quality of Worklife Manager for Westinghouse Electric Corporation's Industry Services Division, and Chicago Staffing Division Chief for the U.S. Office of Personnel Management.

He was a participant in the President's Executive Exchange Program and is a history graduate of the University of California at Berkeley.

Part Two

Understanding Empowerment—What the Experts Say

"Treat people as though they were what they ought to be and you help them become what they are capable of being."

—Goethe

2

Empowerment: There's More to It Than Meets the Eye

by Susan Albers Mohrman, Ph.D.

The term "empowerment" has come to express in many managers' minds the essence of new approaches to management that are believed to be capable of delivering higher levels of performance by tapping into the energies and enthusiasm of employees, and by freeing them from constraints and micro-management. Companies that have tried for years to improve performance through such mechanisms as quality circles, total quality management, employee involvement, and union/management cooperative efforts have discovered that these approaches are more effective when employees have the power to make a difference.

Power is one of the resources (the others being information, knowledge and skills, and rewards) that have to be spread downward in the organization in order to achieve a high involvement system (Lawler, 1992)—i.e., an organization in which employees are involved in the success of the organization. Studies of the quality circle movement have shown that these programs in many cases died out because the circles didn't have the power to make change (e.g., Lawler and Mohrman, 1985). More recently, Peter Block (1990) has popularized the notion of empowerment in his book The Empowered Manager, which describes new ways to manage that change the power dynamics in an organization.

Some large corporations have said their organizational strategy is empowerment. This focus is both laudable and dangerous. It is laudable because it connotes a willingness to reconsider the power dynamics that have perpetuated the status quo and worked against significant organizational change. It is dangerous because we run the risk of management oversimplifying what has to change in order to increase performance. This danger comes from two overly simplistic notions held by some managements:

1) Thinking of empowerment as an individual characteristic that can be achieved by exhorting people to act differently to make decisions and take risks. This overlooks the fact that behavior of people is shaped by organizational practices, structures, policies and systems as well as by people's skills and motivations. This simplistic notion of empowerment can lead to the consoling misconception that people can be empowered without changing anything in the organization.

2) Equating empowerment with "autonomy"—i.e., empowerment occurs when organizational units and people are able to determine what they do and how they do it. In an organizational setting, units are parts of larger wholes that have goals, missions and market imperatives. It is important that empowerment be defined to include organizational direction and to address the question of what people are being empowered to do. Empowerment must be placed in a context of responsibility to the larger whole.

These two partial truths about empowerment are dangerous because they may result in management abdicating its critical role in empowering the organization: to design the organization for empowerment, and to provide direction within which empowered teams and individuals can make a difference. The rest of this chapter addresses the definition of empowerment and several facets of the empowerment concept. It draws implications for organizations that have as part of their strategy the improvement of performance through approaches that require the empowerment of people.

Definition

In an organizational setting, a definition that seems to make sense is: Empowerment is being able to make a difference in the attainment of individual, group, and organizational goals.

This definition acknowledges both organizational and individual purposes. To attract and retain high quality employees, an organization must make it possible for employees to achieve career and professional satisfaction, and to experience intrinsic satisfactions of accomplishment and pride as well as extrinsic satisfactions of reward and recognition. Likewise, to be successful in the market place, the organization must enact a competitive strategy and deliver value.

Empowerment must relate to both the individual goals and the organizational goals. In fact, the concept of organizational empowerment requires that individual and organizational goals are aligned. Otherwise, people will be empowered to do things that are not in the organization's interests; alternatively, people will be empowered to do things in the organization's interest but not motivated to do so because it is not in their own self interest. The human resource systems of the organization are key tools in accomplishing such alignment.

Notions of Empowerment

Several notions of empowerment have appeared in the literature, each of which offers insight into organizational empowerment, and useful direction for organizations. These are briefly described below.

I. Psychological Notions of Empowerment

This view holds that empowerment is the "mind-set" of the person, and relates to notions of assertiveness, efficacy, and self-confidence. It holds that feelings of empowerment stem in part from the natural predisposition of people and in part from years of experience being successful or unsuccessful in accomplishing things and achieving goals.

Studies have demonstrated that it is possible to teach disempowerment—or in other words, for people to learn helplessness. Some classic studies where the concept of learned helplessness was first illustrated involved teaching hungry dogs not to pursue food by putting an electric shock field between the dog and the food. The failure to pursue food generalizes to situations where there is no shock field, as the dog has "learned" to be helpless.

A similar phenomenon seems to occur with people. They learn not to try to accomplish their goals if they repeatedly experience negative consequences as they try to accomplish things. This can lead to a syndrome that is common in many organizations: employees feel that they won't let them do things. The people who are the they—the managers, staff groups, corporate offices, and so forth—are surprised by this impression. They may believe that there are procedures and processes that allow people to get things done. Examining the actual processes, however, yields a whole series of "electric shocks" along the way—paperwork to fill out, cross examinations, huge response delays, having to deal with people who talk down to you as though you don't understand life, and so forth. Ultimately, there is a large possibility that the request will be turned down.

In this kind of environment, people may have stopped trying to get things accomplished, and have come to believe that they can't get things done. This may take the form of "minimalist" behavior—of doing just as much as it takes to get by—or of "testing the limits" in order to accomplish personal goals. In response, management may have put more and more controls in place. This becomes a self-sealing loop.

Related to empowerment is self-efficacy—i.e. the belief in one's ability to successfully accomplish things based on confidence in one's skills and abilities. If people repeatedly apply skills and effort and do not succeed — e.g., in getting a necessary change made or task accomplished—they may develop a lack of self-efficacy. This leads them to stop trying and to avoid challenges. The lack of self-efficacy may be specific to certain kinds of challenges. For example, a person may feel very efficacious in applying professional skills to the task at hand, but not efficacious in dealing with the organization to get needed support and contextual changes. Consequently, the person will concentrate on the task that leads to feeling efficacious, and not worry about the bigger picture.

Taking a psychological view of empowerment puts the emphasis on changes in the mind-set of the individual, and consequently in the way that the individual relates to the organizational context. Thus, practitioners who utilize this framework will help the individual clarify goals, develop knowledge and skills, overcome inertia, and try to make changes. The approach is: don't wait for the context to change; through your own energies, you can create your own context. Organizationally, however, the task is to remove the "electric shocks" that result in a low sense of efficacy.

II. A Sociological View of Empowerment

This approach emphasizes individuals' and groups' abilities to deal with their context. Early work looked at community groups that are disempowered, and at what was necessary for them to become more effective in getting their needs met and building a more positive context for themselves. Behavior is assumed to a great extent to be constrained by context. Power differentials hold the status quo in place, and change requires the utilization of effective influence and power techniques for this to happen. Three components of empowerment are particularly important:

1. Understanding yourself in relation to the context in which you operate: This includes how your goals and aspirations are related to the context, what impact it has on you and what behavior patterns you have been using to cope. For example, you may have given up and withdrawn; you may cope by complaining about the "they" but not try to change things; or you may ignore all the aspects of the context that promote suboptimal performance and concentrate on your

narrow sphere. The belief is that people will be motivated to exert effort to change their context only if they see what's in it for them, such as how their worklife will be improved if they can help make changes and improvements.

2. Understanding the context, and how it operates: People may feel victimized by bureaucracy, perhaps because they don't understand how to make it work for them. People often don't have a picture of the different groups in their organization, where to get information, and what resources are available. The likelihood of having successful impact on an organization increases with an understanding of the organization and how it operates.

3. Skills and Abilities: Making changes and improvements in an organization requires skills and abilities beyond technical job skills. Group process, problem solving, influence and communication are some of the skills for accomplishing personal and organizational goals in a complicated organizational context.

This approach to empowerment has as its goal to teach people to be effective in influencing their organizational context. It assumes that the context will only change if people develop the skills and are motivated to exert effort to change it. Such knowledge and skills development underpins many empowerment-based approaches in organizations.

III. Organizational Design

This way of understanding empowerment focuses on the design of the context itself and how it fosters or impedes people's ability to make a difference. On a global basis, for instance, totalitarian regimes make it difficult for people not in the inner power circle to make a difference in their own daily life and in how the society works. Democratic regimes offer many more opportunities for input and influence. Design features such as electoral procedures, budgeting processes, referenda, and free press build in influence opportunities. The same can be said for different forms of organization. Some organizational features stifle influence and consequently stifle innovation; other features promote opportunities for influence and for innovating and trying different approaches. Some organizations are designed to tightly control behavior from the top and to ensure conformity. Other organizations are designed to control through results, and to promote diversity of practice and innovation.

The organizational design approach to understanding empowerment suggests that organizations can purposefully change aspects of their design in order to promote empowered behavior. For instance, eliminating levels of approval makes it easier to get things done. Levels of approval place a personal cost (time, frustration, delays, impersonal treatment) that make it onerous to do things. Collecting central information but not making information readily available to the people doing the work stifles empowerment. True empowerment can only occur if people are well informed. For people to become involved in improving organizational performance, practices, policies, and organizational design elements must foster such a relationship between people and the organization.

Since organizations have purposes and missions, for people to become involved in making a difference, their efforts must be channeled in the direction of the valued organizational outcomes. Thus, goal-setting and accountability systems are as important to empowerment as influence systems. Furthermore, since the efforts of many groups are often required to succeed in meeting goals, there must be design features such as shared goals that increase the likelihood that various stakeholders work together, and that one stakeholder doesn't ride roughshod over another in the course of exercising empowerment.

Finally, since an organization has to achieve a predictable identity in the marketplace, there will be dimensions of performance and organization that will have to be relatively uniform across units. Consequently, people must be empowered within an overall strategic direction and broad parameters that are common in all units. It is important that those broad parameters and strategic direction have been formulated with the contribution of people and groups who have diverse perspectives, and that there is widespread knowledge and understanding of the direction and common parameters.

Summary: Facets of Empowerment

The notion of empowerment includes a psychological component (people clarifying their goals and developing a sense of efficacy and developing skills); a sociological component (people and groups understanding the context in which they are operating and developing effective influence and power techniques); and an organizational design component (designing the various features of the organization in order to empower people to make a difference).

Empowerment includes both an individual and an organizational focus: people must be empowered to make a difference in their own outcomes as well as in their workgroup's or organization's outcomes. The organization design task is to make sure that these are aligned, i.e. that people are accomplishing their own goals as they contribute to improvement in organizational functioning. Performance management practices such as pay, appraisal and career systems are key design features in creating such alignment.

Because of the purposeful, collective aspects of the organization, there will always be a necessity for a common strategic direction and some aspects of organizational functioning will be common across the organization. Thus, empowerment of subunits (areas, departments, workgroups, individuals) must be within the constraints of common direction and parameters. Even the process used to determine direction and arrive at and improve common parameters can, however, take into account the perspectives of a broad array of stakeholders, increasing the likelihood that people will feel empowered while operating within shared constraints.

The role of management in providing direction, responding to input, designing an organization that facilitates empowerment, and ensuring that individuals and groups have the skills, knowledge and information to effectively utilize power cannot be overestimated. In fact, in an empowered organization, managers' jobs will increasingly consist of designing the context and providing direction within which units can manage more aspects of their own functioning.

Susan Albers Mohrman is a senior research scientist at the Center for Effective Organizations in the School of Business at the University of Southern California. She received her Ph.D. from Northwestern University and her BA from Stanford University. Her career has been spent studying and consulting to the design of high performing systems, including team-based and other lateral designs that operate by creating the conditions for work to get performed laterally. An underpinning of most high performing systems is the creation of an organizational context in which people can be empowered to make decisions and are motivated to make a difference in organizational performance.

She is co-author of nine books, including *Designing Team-Based Organizations* and *Creating High-Performance Organizations: Practices and Results of Employee Involvement and Total Quality Management in Fortune 1000 Companies*, both from Jossey-Bass Publishers in 1995.

References:

Block, Peter. *The Empowered Manager: Positive Political Skills at Work.* San Francisco: Jossey-Bass Publishers, 1990.

Lawler, E.E., III. *The Ultimate Advantage.* San Francisco: Jossey-Bass Publishers, 1992.

Lawler, E.E., III. and Mohrman, S.A., "Quality Circles After the Fad." *Harvard Business Review*, 1985, 85(1), 64-71.

3

Characteristics of An Empowered Organization

by William C. Byham, Ph.D.

Rapidly changing and complex challenges—customer demands, new technologies, global economies, redefined workforce values, and increasingly tougher competitors—make staying ahead in today's work world seem like being in a race that never ends. Many successful organizations have confronted these challenges by questioning and, ultimately, redefining the organization's vision and values. As a result, traditional elements of an organization are evolving. Today's successful organizations are characterized by a flattened management structure, higher ceilings of responsibility, and more accountability on the front lines. But to make things happen—to get employees to embrace change and make it happen—organizations must tap into the basic human needs of pride and achievement.

Organizations that have achieved miracles in quality, customer service, and productivity have done so because their employees possess a sense of job ownership and identification. They work harder and smarter and they seek opportunities for continuous improvement not simply for the good of their organization. They do it because they identify with their jobs and are proud of their successes. The common name for this phenomenon is empowerment.

Empowerment is a feeling of job ownership and commitment brought about through the ability to make decisions, be responsible, be measured by results, and be recognized as a thoughtful, contributing human being rather than as a pair of hands doing what others say. It implies the authority to make decisions, follow through, and get things done. Organizations such as IBM, Hewlett-Packard, and General Electric have proclaimed empowerment the engine that will drive their continuous improvement efforts in quality, customer service, and productivity. They're not alone.

In my consulting work, I can usually identify an empowered organization minutes after I walk through its doors. There's an electricity in the air. People are walking around purposefully. They're interested in what they are doing. There's a sense of achievement and hard work. Most of all, people are happy and enjoying their work.

Characteristics of an Empowered Organization

After visiting hundreds of organizations that are on the journey toward empowerment, I have defined 14 factors that are needed to achieve maximum empowerment. An audit of where an organization stands relative to those factors is a good starting place in creating an empowered organization. No organization will be high in all 14 factors. Even highly competitive organizations can't claim that distinction. These factors are basically goals to be achieved.

    1. **Understanding at all organizational levels the meaning of empowerment and how to achieve it.** Empowerment is a value or belief system, not a program. All levels of the organization must understand how empowerment can meet both personal and business needs and the actions needed to achieve it.

    2. **Well-understood and accepted vision and values to guide decision making.** An empowered organization supports decision making at the level closest to the customer. To make good decisions, people need to have a clear understanding of the organization's direction—its vision—and how they contribute to achieving it. They also need to understand the organization's basic values, which can act as guidelines for decision making.

    3. **Performance management systems that provide a clear understanding of job responsibilities and methods for measuring success.** Empowered employees and leaders work together to devel-

op a clear understanding of job responsibilities, limits of authority, and methods for measuring success. To ensure optimum performance, individuals need to know how their goals and performance expectations link to the overall objectives of the team, the department, and the business strategy of the organization. They also need continuous feedback on their performance, suggestions for improvement, and coaching for success.

At Trane Co. in LaCrosse, Wisconsin, their empowerment strategy meshes with the entire management process, which also includes quality programs and a demand-flow process that allows workers latitude in making decisions about what they should be working on. As a result, the organization has become more streamlined, with fewer managers and employees who shoulder greater responsibility.

4. Jobs designed to provide ownership and responsibility. Empowerment must be built into employees' jobs. Tasks must be defined so that people with responsibility for a meaningful process or output can make decisions, commit appropriate organizational resources, and continually measure their own successes. Empowered employees have the time, knowledge and resources to achieve success.

At Development Dimensions International's printing and distribution facility, empowered employee teams do their own budgeting and negotiate the purchasing of supplies and high cost equipment. Not only have they saved the company thousands of dollars, these empowered employees share a sense of pride and accomplishment in their work.

The following examples illustrate some traditional management responsibilities that organizations have shifted to employees in empowered teams. Each is proof that empowerment strategies are reaping benefits in terms of employee satisfaction and gaining a competitive edge.

— At Aid Association for Lutherans (AAL), teams do their own interviewing and make hiring decisions.

— At a Colgate-Palmolive plant in Ohio, empowered employees design their own technical training manuals.

— At Lake Superior Paper Industries, teams of employees handle their own work scheduling, work assignments, and holiday and vacation planning.

— At Johnsonville Foods, a sausage company in Sheboygan, Wisconsin, whose sales skyrocketed from $4 million to $150 million as they embarked on an eight-year journey to self-direction, the company was presented with a lucrative opportunity to produce sausage for an outside company on a special basis. The managers were concerned that the large order would hurt current production schedules and affect quality. However, highly committed to empowerment, employee team members decided to "go for it," scheduled the work, upheld quality standards, and gained an opportunity to learn how to handle larger volumes of work successfully.

5. **Effective communication about the organization's plans, successes, and failures.** Empowered people are "in the know" about the organization's plans, successes, and failures. Truthful and up-to-date communication ensures that employees identify with the organization and actively contribute to its success. When employees understand the organization's direction, they're more likely to support its actions.

6. **Reward and recognition systems that build pride and self-esteem.** Empowered employees have an inherent sense of pride in their accomplishments and contributions to the organization. Psychological and tangible recognition programs can enhance these feelings. Compensation and other reward systems need to be in sync with the empowered organization's values. Often these systems need to become more team-oriented in their recognition of job performance and specific accomplishments.

7. **Selection and promotion systems to identify quality workers and leaders.** Some people are more interested than others in becoming empowered. Placing individuals with appropriate motivations and skills in an empowered environment increases the likelihood that the benefits of empowerment will be achieved in a more timely and cost-effective manner. Also, an organization's selection and promotion choices can communicate its commitment to

empowerment.

As an organization moves toward empowerment, the required dimensions or competencies of an employee change a great deal. As a matter of fact, those dimensions look more like dimensions of a traditional supervisor, and the dimensions of a supervisor in an empowered organization reflect the dimensions of a traditional manager. Faced with these differences in hiring specifications, organizations have developed significantly different methodologies for hiring employees and managers. They realize that they can't assume that employees are interchangeable parts, but instead, are long-term investments in which a lot of time, money, and training will be devoted.

8. Organizational systems such as information systems and travel-reimbursements policies. Other organizational systems—information systems, travel-reimbursement policies, career-planning procedures, succession planning, discipline, personnel policies, tuition refund policy, quality circles, suggestion systems—can either instill people with a sense of power or make them feel as if they have none.

9. Empowering leadership/training. Leaders have tremendous impact on the degree of empowerment their employees feel. Through the tasks they delegate, the control they exert, the initiative they encourage, and the feedback and reinforcement they provide, empowering leaders not only encourage empowerment but build employee confidence. By coaching for success and helping employees feel ownership for their ideas, leaders ensure employees' dedication and commitment to their work. Enhancement of leadership skills is an ongoing process as employees and teams move toward increased empowerment.

At Frisch's Restaurants Inc., good employee relations are being nurtured by a management strategy that focuses on giving employees more responsibility in the decision-making process. Since they implemented an empowerment program in 1991, the Cincinnati-based restaurant chain has seen earnings jump and company-wide performance improve significantly. Frisch's managers attend day-

long training sessions each quarter where they are encouraged to use DDI's four Key Principles of Empowerment:
- Maintain or enhance self-esteem
- Listen and respond with empathy
- Ask for help and encourage involvement
- Offer help without taking responsibility for action.

10. Job and technical skills/training. In an empowered organization, employees tackle additional tasks and often rotate jobs. They need to understand how to do not only their own jobs, but every job on their team. They might be required to learn statistical process control or their company's budgetary process. Technical and job training prepares employees for these new responsibilities. Nothing is more empowering than providing employees with skills training to do their jobs well.

11. Interpersonal and problem-solving skills/training. Empowered employees, as individuals or in teams, interact more often with co-workers, suppliers, customers, and management. They are expected to identify problems and opportunities and take appropriate actions. Empowered employees must be able to lead others and resolve their own conflicts without appealing to higher authority. Skills training usually is needed as employees and teams assume more responsibilities.

Organizations where problem-solving/skills training has gone hand-in-hand to support empowerment include: General Motors, American Express, Harris Corporation, Litton Guidance & Control Systems, Texas Instruments, Unisys Corporation, General Foods Corporation, and hundreds more.

12. Front-line customer service skills/training. Empowered organizations focus on customer service skills because their front-line people represent the organization to the customer. Customers' perceptions of an organization develop from the treatment they receive from customer-contact people. Empowered organizations such as BP America, Rockwell International, and Procter & Gamble have provided the training front-line service people need to meet and exceed their customers' expectations.

13. Empowering support groups/training. Like leaders, support group personnel—engineering, accounting, training—can help front-line employees build a sense of job ownership and responsibility. Ongoing training and management support are required to help them assume these new roles. Support personnel who effectively coach, reinforce, and offer help without taking responsibility build employee confidence and skill. Empowered employees gradually handle more of the support groups' responsibilities. Ultimately, an effective support group evolves from doers into trainers and coaches, viewing others as their partners.

14. Work teams. More and more, organizations empower by encouraging teams and teamwork—cross-functional quality action teams, customer focus groups, and integrated product development teams. A special type of team—the empowered work team—organizes individuals so that they are responsible for a given area or output. The team takes on many responsibilities assigned previously to supervisors, such as job assignments, product quality, selection of new team members, and sometimes even performance evaluation. An empowered work team is an excellent way of empowering individuals whose current jobs are limited in scope.

Hannaford Brothers Company, a retail supermarket and food distribution company, began its empowerment journey in 1989. Within a couple of years, empowered teams were responsible for inventory control, peer performance reviews, scheduling work assignments, and team budgeting. As a result, they are in the top 15 percent of cost-efficient distribution centers nationwide and fewer on-the-job injuries reduced worker compensation costs by $500,000.

Miller Brewing Company developed its first empowered teams in 1991. All 410 of its employees at the Trenton, Ohio plant are now working in teams. They hire, conduct peer performance assesments, assure safety, maintain equipment and much more. As a result, Miller has seen a 30% reduction in labor costs and a corresponding increase in productivity.

Is empowerment worth the effort? Both from my consulting in this area and from applications of empowerment within our own

1,200-person organization, I can tell you that empowerment does work and brings with it substantial improvements in quality, customer service, and productivity. Most important, empowerment evokes a whole new employee attitude. For that reason alone, empowerment is worth the effort. But you've got to see it to believe it.

William C. Byham is co-founder, chief executive officer and president of Development Dimensions International, a leading human resource assessment, training and organizational change provider with corporate headquarters in Pittsburgh, Pennsylvania. An internationally known businessman, educator, and author, Bill has written more than 200 articles and books. His books on empowerment include: *Zapp! The Lightning of Empowerment; Empowered Teams: Creating Self-Directed Work Groups That Improve Quality, Productivity; and Participation*; and *Heroz: Empower Yourself, Your Coworkers, Your Company*. All books are available from DDI at 1-800-933-4463.

4

Defining the Boundaries of Empowerment

by Ken Somers, Ph.D.

"We need empowered people. Dedicated and energetic people who always seize the initiative, but only when appropriate. People who take risks, but never risky ones. People who volunteer ideas, but only brilliant ones. People who solve problems on their own, but never make mistakes."

Empowerment. The word has entered our business language as yet another term casually used to describe something that enlightened managers do for. . . or to. . . employees. It's the new mantra, but what is it? How does it work? How do you move it from buzzword to reality?

Why is empowerment so elusive? There are several fundamental barriers to successful empowerment. First, many who use the term don't define it. They don't understand what it means to empower. Well-intentioned leaders block empowerment by sending conflicting signals. Many traditional organizations resist empowerment through their structures and command-control processes. Add these together, and empowerment translates poorly from theory to practice.

But that doesn't have to be the case. As a leader, you can "operationalize" empowerment by understanding its boundaries and the role you play to empower others. Let's begin with a definition.

What is Empowerment?

A simple, straight-forward definition of empowerment is, "To provide with the means and opportunity to make decisions and take actions which directly affect the customer."

This definition *sounds* reasonable, but to operationalize it, look beyond the words. Empowerment is difficult to achieve because we tend to oversimplify the concept. Plainly put, we talk about it without really thinking through what the definition means.

Think for a moment about your personal definition of empowerment. Do you have one? Can you articulate it clearly? Would you stumble for a definition if put on the spot by a skeptical employee? Are you able to describe exactly what you mean when you say you want to empower people?

This is particularly important for leaders. Followers base a tremendous portion of your credibility on your ability to speak plainly, to help them visualize what you have in mind when you talk. If you want to empower people, it's important to develop a definition you believe in, and to teach it to others.

For a start, let's analyze our definition—"To provide with the means and opportunity to make decisions and take actions which directly affect the customer"—phrase by phrase:

"To provide…" implies to give. Empowerment is a gift from leaders to followers. Empowerment is neither assumed nor forfeited. It is transferred via an orderly process that includes a clear statement of expectations and responsibilities.

"The means…" implies a need for training. Empowering the unskilled is doomed to failure. Investment in training is necessary for people to understand fully the scope and limits of their empowerment and the tools, techniques and processes they need to master.

"And opportunity…" implies that you will turn over the reins to those whom you have empowered. At first, you may monitor progress, but empowerment without true authority is simply delegation. People understand being second-guessed.

"To make decisions and take actions…" implies that empowered people have the information, knowledge and decision-making authority to choose the best course of action. Training and latitude are implied if decisions will be made by people other than the traditional decision makers.

"Which directly affect the customer," says the customer is the focus. These words separate empowerment from delegation and participation. If you're willing to allow your employees the power to make decisions and take actions which directly affect the customer, you are ready for empowerment.

A definition is only as good as your ability to demonstrate and teach it. You know the power of "walking the talk," but don't discount "talking the talk." Set the vision for your organization by clearly and concisely describing what the future looks like. Be able to describe what empowerment means to you personally when you empower others. Describe what you expect and how you expect it. Successfully articulating a clear vision and definition is the first step to setting the boundaries of empowerment.

What Empowerment is Not

Some people confuse empowerment with other behaviors, both positive and negative. To be clear on what empowerment is, we must get clear on what empowerment is not. Empowerment is not:

- Indiscriminate assignment of work. That's *dumping*.
- Appointing someone as your representative. That's *delegation*.
- Allowing discretionary power without boundaries. That's *anarchy*.
- Employees replacing managers. Those are *different roles and issues*.
- Asking people to help and be involved in your decisions. That's *participative management*.

Knowing what empowerment is and is not is important. Without clear definitions and appropriate behavior, you may try to empower but only alienate by sending conflicting signals. The first behavior you can control when you seek to empower is your own, so look first at the role of the empowering leader.

The Role of the Leader

Leaders blaze trails, aim their people in the right direction, help them chart unexplored territory. Leaders understand the loose-tight ratio of control, how many boundaries to impose, and the freedom required for followers to seek creative ways to challenge current processes.

Empowering leaders build environments of loose-tight boundary control. First, develop a leadership team which has the same self-awareness and sensitivity to control so that the message from the top is consistent. Seek leadership team members who are willing to give up authority when possible and modulate their personal control. Strive to know the difference between control and over-control, when to intervene, and when to let people exercise full authority.

Second, empower the culture through organizational design. The fewer the layers, the less is lost in translation. Process-focused organizations empower people to focus on the customer. Traditional hierarchies encourage people to focus on the boss.

Third, monitor empowerment through feedback. The business enterprise is dynamic, not static. The degrees of freedom required by the organization today will likely be different tomorrow. Formal and informal lines of feedback keep track of organizational dynamics and leadership adjustments required.

Fourth, set boundaries of empowerment. Define the terms and conditions of empowerment so everyone understands the rules of the game. Then, play by the rules. Stay within the boundaries you help set to demonstrate your commitment to and trust in empowered people.

Why Boundaries are Important

Boundaries are important because they define the roles and responsibilities and the degrees of freedom for all the participants—leaders and followers—in the empowered culture.

A frequent pitfall occurs when leaders oversimplify empowerment, and dismiss the hard work that is necessary to empower people. This happens because leaders, who are empowered by position, overlook the constraints under which the rest of the organization toils.

Followers work within systems of disempowerment, both real and perceived, which inhibit their span of control and decision authority. Work through the boundaries and set mutually agreed-upon expectations to manage empowered behavior for results.

Defining the Boundaries

What are the boundaries of empowerment and how do leaders set them? Think of empowered behavior as a territory with four boundaries. As leaders blaze trails through the territory, they take with them the people who map the territory and manage its resources. Before beginning the journey and while en route, leaders work closely with the team to define the boundaries of acceptable actions and decisions—the authority, responsibility and accountability of all team members—within a common reference of empowered behavior.

The four boundaries of empowered behavior are Span of Control, Resource Control, Decision Authority, and Mutual Trust. Work through these boundaries with your people to ensure that the terms and conditions of empowerment are well communicated throughout the organization; that roles and responsibilities are clearly understood. Following are some ways to do that.

Span of Control

Span of control is about processes. It is the boundary which defines the start points, stop points, deliverables and relationships of the processes managed by the empowered person or group. Defining the span of control is important so that as people expand their authority and decision making, they do so in harmony with other processes and people.

The role of the leader is to jointly define the span of control with the empowered people. Facilitate a discussion to:

Define the Process

Process start and stop points
    Define process receivables and deliverables
Process capability
    Determine what is required and what is possible
Relationships desired
    At each customer-supplier link
Supplier capabilities
    Link suppliers to your strategic vision
Define the process contribution
    Search for opportunities for improvement
    Plan for and prioritize improvements

Span of control is a loose-tight criterion, meaning that it's necessary to encourage people to exercise control over an ever-broadening sphere of influence, but to acknowledge and respect the point at which authority belongs elsewhere.

Resource Control

Resource control is about cost and investment. It is the boundary which sets the time, people and money necessary to meet the requirements established in the span of control discussion.

Resource control is a tight issue, but *determining* resource requirements is loose-tight. Here, the role of the leader is to allow freedom for others to set the resource allocation, within limits, and then to hold them accountable to their plan. Facilitate a discussion to:

Define the Contribution Expected

    Financial contribution/what is at risk
    Dollar value of corrective/preventive action

Define the Resources Required
Time
People
Operating budget
Confirm the return on investment

Set Milestones for Control
Measures
Key dates and contribution levels
Alternative plans

The sophistication and experience of those whom you empower will determine the resource control required. Resource control provides an excellent framework to train people on key financial drivers and set cost of quality and contribution objectives linked to the strategic plan.

Decision Authority

Decision authority is the most telling empowerment boundary. The authority given, and an employee's ability to make decisions and take action without management approval are the true tests of empowerment. Second-guess employees, and empowerment is lost. Co-decide all issues, and you are practicing involvement, not empowerment. If you can't let go of authority, and can't trust your people to best manage the enterprise, you are not ready for empowerment. When you empower, you entrust authority to others.

Decision models are useful tools for setting authority. Models which guide the decision-making process include key questions such as:

1. Who is accountable for this decision?
2. What is the level of authority required?
3. Who will be affected?
4. Are others required to make this decision?
5. Does the situation require a command or consensus decision?

6. What is the time allowed to reach a decision?
7. To whom will the decision be elevated if a decision cannot be reached within the allocated time?

Answering these questions early-on helps the leader set ground rules for decision-making and avoid misunderstandings. Since people will be held personally accountable for their decisions, it is important to have a systematic process in place which provides the opportunity to foresee outcomes and guide the decision process in advance of results.

Recognize the richness of the decision making process and build a culture where each style can contribute. A value in empowering others to decide and act is that you distribute your decision risk by drawing on the varied styles of many instead of becoming locked into your own singular approach. But while you can benefit from diversity, you can suffer from it as well. To minimize the risks associated with diversified authority, establish decision ownership and levels in advance.

Mutual Trust

Mutual trust is the fourth boundary of empowerment. It builds gradually throughout the empowerment process, and cements the other boundaries. People will be skeptical of empowerment when you introduce it formally. Past practices, over-controlling managers and the old reward systems warrant skepticism. The role of the leader is to anticipate and manage skepticism, eventually extinguishing it through demonstrated commitment to and practice of empowerment.

Trust is another word which is used casually, but one which should be defined carefully. Trust is the confidence earned by people who make and keep agreements. Leaders earn trust when they keep the agreement of empowerment, not when they promise it.

To build mutual trust, work with your people to define empowerment and its boundaries. Set the span of control, and respect the authority and decision making agreements. Trust those closest to the work to manage resources without second-guessing them.

Managing the Empowerment Process

The way that empowerment is managed is just as important as the leader's vision of empowerment. There are six key management systems which you can use to ensure that empowerment is brought to each management action. The systems are planning, involvement, communication, review, accountability and recognition.

These systems define the job of management, and, if used to operationalize empowerment, will demonstrate that you are sincere about keeping the agreement to empower others. To use the management systems, ask yourself questions such as these:

Planning: What is the objective?

How does it support the mission?

How will empowering others to act benefit the organization and help achieve the mission?

Whom do I need to empower, and to what extent?

Involvement: Who should be involved in this venture?

How do I ask for their involvement?

How will I define the boundaries of empowerment? What input will I seek and provide?

Communication: How do I describe the mission linkage?

What do others need and want to know?

How will I solicit and provide ideas, feedback and input?

What will be the lines of communication between me and those empowered?

What information needs to be shared, and when?

Accountability: Who will be accountable for meeting the objectives?

What are my responsibilities to help them define and understand their accountability?

Review: Who is responsible for review?

How will we review progress toward the goal?

What are the key milestones and performance measures?

Recognition: What is the appropriate recognition for success?

When will the recognition be done?

Who is responsible for recognition?

Organizational systems, including these management systems, can be used to support disempowerment, through the traditional command-and-control process. The leader's role is to challenge the systems which support the traditional methods. You have a choice to use the management systems to foster empowerment, or to extinguish it. All that is required is a change in perspective.

The challenge will be strong. Traditional cultures naturally resist empowerment. Empowerment, and your change in perspective, will be greeted with great skepticism. Managers will rightfully suspect that empowerment is the current buzz-word or program of the month. Employees will be skeptical because they know from past experience the behaviors and results that are rewarded and those which are not. Business-as-usual may appear to be much more comfortable.

People may not understand how to behave in an empowered manner. This is especially true in the transitional organization, where command-and-control has been the norm. The leader's task is to stay the course. Model empowered behavior by helping others take control of their own piece of the enterprise.

Empowerment Pitfalls

Empowerment frequently fails because leaders often become isolated from their own past experience. They forget what it's like to be in other organizational perspectives, on the bottom, looking up, or in the middle, looking both ways. They become accustomed to being empowered, calling the shots and assuming authority.

People display various organizational behaviors, depending upon how they are wired-up naturally, and how they have adapted to the existing culture. For those employees naturally inclined to make decisions and take action, who are already working in an empowered culture, your efforts to define and provide empowerment will be reassuring. But for others, it may be confusing.

It is too easy to say that all employees are empowered. This is neither practically nor realistically true in most organizations. *The secret is that all employees should be empowered within limits commensurate with their level of capability and the situations they generally encounter.* The leader should assess both these criteria—capability and situation—before promising empowerment.

The leader who simply says, "You are empowered! Just do what you have to do to get the job done!" is overlooking his development responsibility for those whom he has "empowered." Saying people are empowered doesn't make it so.

As leader, it's necessary to paint the vision of empowerment and agree on the specifics which define empowered behavior. Model the way by staying the course, and allow the empowered organization the freedom to grow and develop. As the organization progresses, lessen control. Hold people accountable for empowered behavior. Dismantle disempowering processes and structures.

Know the capability, skills and knowledge of your people as you embark on the empowerment journey. Position empowerment situationally. Practice loose-tight control. Get feedback on how it's going, and adjust your style accordingly. *Above all, start with a definition you understand and can teach, and work with your people to establish clear boundaries.*

Wise leaders know that this process takes time. While we can declare empowerment immediately, the transformation to a fully-empowered culture is a gradual process, replete with communications, involvement and constant reinforcement. Back-track often to re-establish the way, because the underbrush will creep back over the trail. Before the trail to empowerment is firm, it will have to be blazed many times.

Ken Somers is founder and principal of J.K. Somers & Associates in Bellaire, Texas. His consulting work spans manufacturing, energy, biotechnology, R&D, utilities, defense contracting, construction, food processing, ship building, paper making, packaging, printing, laboratories, automotive, high technology, electrical apparatus remanufacturing, and environmental engineering.

His technical expertise includes self-managed team development, total quality management, ISO 9000, QS 9000, ISO 14000, process reengineering, customer-supplier strategic alliances and statistical applications.

Before entering consulting, Ken served as Director of Organizational Development and Quality for Duchossois Industries, Director of Sales Development for AM International, and Senior Planner for Tenneco Energy. In addition, Ken has served on the faculty of Bowling Green State University and Texas A&M University. Ken holds a Ph.D. in Industrial Technology and Education from Texas A&M University with advanced training in applied statistics for manufacturing and research.

5

Empowerment Roles and Behaviors

"What should executives, middle managers, supervisors, employees and union leaders do—and avoid doing—to make empowerment successful?" That's the question that was put to 300-plus attendees at the June 1993 Quality & Productivity Management Association conference in San Antonio, which focused on empowerment. Here's their collective answer.

Executives

Role: Proactively champion effective change in their organization. Provide guidance via clearly articulated vision and strategies. Effectively orchestrate a network of (empowered) employees focused on routinely exceeding the needs of key stakeholders.

Behaviors:
Do

Set High Expectations
- Self (personal growth)
- Direct reports
- Service to customers
- Employees

Communicate Frequently & Consistently
- Discuss reasoning behind vision, strategies & key goals
- Review results & progress
- Demonstrate change through personnel actions

- Discuss process daily
- Encourage responsibility, action & total system understanding
- Trust employees (value them)
- Emphasize needs of customers
- Listen with an open (vs. all-knowing) mind
- Spend time outside of office (with customers, employees, suppliers)
- Set clear organizational boundaries and metrics
- Foster ownership
- Make tough decisions regarding
    - Organization structure
    - Behaviors/actions that are not in alignment
- Admit mistakes and move forward
- Recognize appropriate behaviors & results
- Encourage and coach employees
- Accept coaching from others (request honest feedback)
- Prioritize strategies and provide resources
- Use data for decisions and share with others
- Give meaning to the work people do; don't waste it!

Avoid Doing
- Take self too seriously
- Micro-manage
- Announce & disappear
- Dictate empowerment
- Be inconsistent (send mixed signals)
- Punish failure
- Delegate to Quality Assurance or Human Resources
- Abdicate (give up too soon)
- Be overly concerned about slow initial progress
- Ignore results

- Be afraid to make decisions
- Delude yourself into thinking you understand customers or employees better than they understand themselves
- Expect results tomorrow
- Assume you add value
- Bad-mouth internal or external customers
- Have internal competition for rewards
- Just talk about it

Middle Management

Role: In an effort to develop and support a culture of empowerment, middle managers act to effectively facilitate and direct information and work flow throughout the organization. They serve as leaders and role models for others through their efforts to integrate and align the various teams' and work units' goals and objectives with the organization's overall business plan.

Behaviors:

Do

- Enable contribution and implement recommendations
- Recognize & reward risk-taking/innovation and allow for failures; share successes
- Solicit feedback & listen
- Align goals and objectives
- Lead and facilitate
- Provide and support training, develop potential, self-develop
- Be fair, equitable and consistent
- Excite people

Avoid Doing

- Being wishy-washy
- Shooting the messenger
- Controlling

- Getting in the way (not letting the team do it/develop)
- "Black-holing" information
- Withholding information
- Attempting to know it all/have all the answers
- Micro-manage
- Taking control back after empowering
- Criticizing ideas and suggestions
- Being afraid to lose a star (key player)
- Avoiding issues

Supervisors/Coaches

Role: Facilitate their team's alignment with the strategic direction of the organization by communicating and clarifying the vision, values, and goals; by providing guidance, feedback, reward and recognition for expected behavior; and by empowering the team through tools and training.

Behaviors:

Do

- Create excitement by acting as a coach and a cheer leader
- Serve as a role model for interpersonal skills by effectively communicating through verbal and non-verbal cues
- Provide open and direct communication
- Encourage two-way communication by asking questions and by actively listening
- Share information up, down, and sideways
- Catch someone doing something right and recognize them immediately
- Create an environment that engenders respect, trust, and participation
- Keep people focused on the process
- Establish measurement systems

Avoid Doing

- Criticize or condemn through either verbal or non-verbal cues
- Discourage participation in problem solving or process improvement by "doing it yourself," or dictating "how to do it"
- Rule by fear
- Stress personal competition over teamwork

Employees/Associates

Role: To support aggressively the organization's mission and goals (e.g., customer satisfaction and profit) by initiating improvement and taking risks. Employees should collaborate enthusiastically in an open supportive manner and reinforce those behaviors in others.

Behaviors:

Do

- Get excited about the opportunity
- Become educated cross-functionally
- Know when to ask for information or help
- Become committed to the effort; ownership
- Take initiative for improvement, participate
- Be flexible and adapt; willing to change
- Challenge current processes; take risks
- Take responsibility for personal development
- Develop an understanding and focus on customer
- Recognize the contribution of others
- Learn from mistakes; self-correcting, accountable
- Have fun; keep your family first

Avoid Doing

- Sub-optimizing one priority over others

- Pessimism regarding the opportunity
- Counter-productive interpersonal behavior, e.g. belittling, attacking, jealousy, hidden agendas
- Isolating management from the discussion
- Complacency and satisfaction with status quo
- Group think, a "herd" mentality
- Rejection of peer and manager feedback
- Absenteeism, laziness and failure to participate
- "We" vs. "them" attitude toward other teams or departments
- Taking the job for granted
- Careless overstepping of boundaries
- Undermining organization mission or goals

Union Leadership

Role: Work as equal partners with management to create a mutually-beneficial vision, strategy and business objective. Understand the stakes are the same for management, labor and clients.

Behaviors:

Do

- Be realistic about current environmental/business factors affecting the organization
- Be visionary for greater possibilities
- Ensure management understands the union's legal requirement to represent its constituents
- Work for alternative ways to re-deploy people vs. eliminate jobs
- Use problem-solving as a mechanism to achieve win-win
- Walk the talk
- Recognize humanistic ways to reduce the workforce when required...add value to people
- Get involved in how your constituents are trained

- Continue to represent constituents in traditional ways, but shift part of your focus to the ultimate customer
- Get involved in designing empowerment up front
- Anticipate the effects of globalization on jobs & your constituents
- Communicate, communicate, communicate

Avoid Doing
- Corruption
- Political games
- Re-election motivation
- People as a "resource"—add the "resource" to people to empower/develop them
- Letting the past influence your current decisions
- Using teamwork as a negotiating ploy
- Quid-pro-quo; go for win-win bargaining
- "Us vs. them" mentality
- Not be a management tool to de-certify union
- Using empowerment to eliminate union jobs

6

Preparing Supervisors and Employees for Empowerment

by John R. Dew, Ed.D.

This chapter focuses on preparing supervisors to become empowering leaders, and on preparing employees to assume the broader responsibilities incumbent with empowerment. The chapter is based on practices in Lockheed Martin's Energy and Environment sector and in other companies and public sector organizations.

Lockheed Martin gives its business units latitude to explore and invent empowering processes that fit the specific business sectors. Empowerment efforts in this sector have included the formation of teams in which supervisors have become facilitators, the creation of self-managed teams, and the establishment of many project teams.

Empowerment Cannot Be Forced

One of the first lessons in preparing people for empowerment is that people cannot be forced to be empowered. It simply does not work for a manager to one day decide that the workers will be empowered, make an announcement, and expect that decades of behavior will change overnight.

To be empowered, people need to learn concepts and skills that support empowered behavior. The concepts and skills are almost identical for the supervisors who need to become empowering leaders and the workforce that needs to become empowered employees. There is little need to develop a separate curriculum for the supervisors and the general workforce since the path they both follow is very similar. The difference is in the timing, not the content. The supervisors should be ahead of the employees' learning curve if they expect to be able to lead. Empowering leaders need to have a greater depth of learning about the concepts and skills in order to effectively serve as guides.

Some organizations invest in teaching the empowering skills, such as group dynamics, conflict resolution, decision making, and problem solving, without first teaching the concept of empowerment. Skills that are taught without a conceptual base will only be partially utilized. Organizations should start by teaching the concepts of empowerment, and then provide people with the necessary tools to implement.

Teaching the Concepts

Teaching empowerment concepts is a tricky business. The teaching process itself cannot be autocratic, but must be participative. People learn best to become participative through participative educational processes. You cannot instruct other people into becoming empowered.

This means that the educational process should not be based on lecture, but rather on a structured form of discovery in which people participate in role playing and discussion that permits them to make their own discovery about empowerment. The opposite of empowerment, whether in the work place or the classroom, is usually endullment: a condition in which people feel they have no control over their work or their learning, leading to apathy.

Successful empowerment efforts begin by conducting workshops where people discover that empowerment works and that the results of an empowered work setting are superior to the results of non-participative management. This is usually accomplished by conducting role playing exercises in which participants perform work in a highly structured endulling setting and analyze the negative results of autocratic control on their own morale and productivity. The work conditions in the role playing exercise are then altered to empower the participants to make decisions, with typical improvements in morale and productivity.

The individual's discovery of the benefits of empowerment is then reinforced from numerous case studies developed over the last 50 years that offer objective evidence of the superior performance of empowered work organizations over autocratic organizations. A transformation occurs when people have personally experienced the contrast of autocratic and empowering conditions and can then review corroborating evidence from numerous studies that prove superior performance occurs in organizations that have chosen to empower their workforces.

Other educational methods can be used to supplement role playing and case studies. Adults respond well to discussion questions that allow them to analyze the various aspects of empowerment, such as the five concepts in the following section titled "Bottom Line Concepts for Empowerment." Discussion questions about each of the concepts can be offered in a workshop setting where people have the opportunity to discuss the concepts with their peers and to hear what their peers think about empowerment.

There are also some excellent video case studies available for use in training sessions that will spark discussion and analysis. Marvin Weisbord's Blue Sky Productions has created video case studies that offer insights into the dynamics of empowered work teams and that help managers deal with their changing roles in an empowerment effort.

Some adults learn best through the written word, so a workshop on empowerment concepts should always provide articles or case studies for people to read on their own. There are many excellent articles in the quality literature and several good case studies and reports in the last few years of the *Harvard Business Review* that can be purchased for use.

Benchmarking offers another powerful method for educating people about the power of empowerment. When people are benchmarking an empowerment effort in another organization, they often do not know what to expect, so it is difficult for them to prepare specific questions to ask. So, while there may not be a lot of preparation that people can do beforehand, there should be a clear plan in place for providing a debriefing time, or an opportunity to sit down and process what people saw during the benchmarking.

Combining these methods into a unique program can be most effective for an organization. A workshop that includes role playing and case studies can be reinforced with top-notch reading materials, and then made real by a benchmarking visit to an empowered organizational setting, capped off by a planning process back home on how to implement.

Team-building as Education

Some forms of team-building offer another opportunity for people to discover the power of empowerment. Many organizations attempt to improve performance by organizing the workforce into teams. Sometimes this is done with a clear desire to create an empowered workforce, and sometimes it is done as simply a copycat action. In either case, the structural creation of teams can set the stage for empowerment with the right kind of team-building process.

As discussed above, effective team-building first focuses on concepts before working on skill building. Without the concepts, the skills will never be fully utilized. The team can work on concepts through exercises that cause team members to reflect on how they work together. Group exercises that foster reflection can be structured and taught in a team-building session.

One approach that has proven to be successful within Lockheed Martin is to challenge a team to examine itself as if it were a sports team. If the team were evaluated as a basketball team, for instance, how would one define the roles of the team members? What are the rules that the team members are playing by? What is the team's equivalent of a foul, or double dribbling, or a three-point score? What are some examples of games the team has clearly won? What were the conditions in effect when the team won? How did they play together and support each other? What are examples of when the team lost a game? How did their teamwork differ in the losing game from the winning game? What, then, are the conditions the team needs for success?

Bottom Line Concepts for Empowerment

Here are the concepts that people need to discover in their workshops or team-building exercises that will cause them to value empowerment and want to learn the skills necessary for working in an empowered setting.

1. Success depends on having a *common sense of mission and goals* that everyone in the organization supports. Support for goals comes from participation in setting the goals.
2. All organizations have *boundaries* that are clearly established and maintained. An autocratic organization has tight boundaries that confine people and cause them to become endulled. An empowering organization expands the boundaries, giving people more control over their situations. Boundaries and accountability must be linked at all times.
3. The *roles* within a work group must be defined. They can be rotated, shared, or divided up into specialized jobs, but all the necessary roles need to be executed. People need to acknowledge the roles. Expanding people's control over deciding how the roles will be carried out is a significant act of empowerment.
4. *Consensus decision making* is valuable for group cohesion and commitment to goals. Leaders challenge the group to set high goals.
5. Empowered work groups, or teams, need constant feedback through *performance indicators* that tell them how they are doing in terms of customer expectations, internal goals, and day-to-day performance. Information generates knowledge and knowledge is power, since it enables people to make effective decisions.

Skill Building for Empowerment

Once the empowerment concepts are in place, people are ready to start implementing and working as empowered team players. In some organizations, this just seems to occur naturally, since people are already well educated and have the skills necessary to work with newly expanded boundaries.

In other organizations, training and education will be historically weak, so people will need to develop new skills in order to successfully function as empowered employees. The needs for each organization are unique, so the organization should conduct a needs analysis to determine where to place its training emphasis.

In general, there are six areas in which people need to be adequately educated and trained in order to function effectively in an empowered manner.

1. Technical Knowledge

The technical tasks that are performed by a work team or individual should be listed, and the skills required for each task should be listed alongside the task. This list can then be used to create a matrix that defines the task, the training required to perform the task, and whether or not each team member has the training and skill to perform the task. Once this matrix is prepared, team members can cross train one another, or the team leader can assume the role of trainer.

With a task and training matrix prepared, new team members can be quickly brought up to speed in their work performance. The task and training matrix can become one of the team's performance indicators for tracking team success.

2. Team Process Skills

In an empowering work setting, people need skills to function well in a team environment. This includes understanding the life cycle of groups, team-based decision making, planning skills, the effective use of performance indicators, and how to run a team meeting.

All of these skills can be taught in brief modules by a facilitator or trainer. Outside organizations, such as community colleges, consultants, and training vendors offer a wide variety of courses to teach these skills.

The important thing is to begin with a needs assessment. What have we already taught the workforce in prior training programs? For example, there is no sense teaching performance indicators if people already have them and know how to use them.

Like the empowerment concepts, team process skills cannot be taught in a lecture setting, so beware of vendors who want to sell some type of complete package of training. Team skills need to be taught in workshops where people can practice the concepts and discuss how applying these skills will impact their group's performance.

3. Interpersonal Skills

Most work groups profit from at least a small investment in training related to interpersonal skills. This can be training that points out the differences in personality profiles of team members, training on conflict resolution, or training on effective living skills.

An organization should select one personality profile tool and stick to it across the board, not allowing multiple tools to proliferate. Standardization provides lower costs in training and consistency of language across the organization, leading to synergy from the training. Most tools have an evaluation mechanism in which other people fill out an assessment profile about a team member. The profile is completed and tabulated, usually by an outside organization, and then shared with the team members in a facilitated group setting. When team members better understand their own personality, and the personality of other team members, communication, cooperation, and understanding are enhanced.

Similarly, training in conflict resolution can be very useful and can be obtained from a variety of sources. If a team is struggling with conflicts that threaten to tear it apart (often the residual of the bad old days of endullment), it may be advisable to bring in a professional counselor to help the group sort through issues.

Teams often benefit from training that focuses on effective living skills, such as stress management, creative thinking, and clarifying life issues. Stephen Covey's workshop on The 7 Habits of Highly Effective People is being used in Lockheed Martin as both a standard course in professional development and a tool for fostering teamwork in empowered work settings.

4. Business Knowledge

In an empowered organization, management needs to "open the books" to educate the workforce about the economic realities of their work environment. This process should cover broad issues, such as who the organization's international competition may be, as well as specific issues, such as what this year's plant budget looks like and what the budget for each specific work team may be. Control of costs should be a performance indicator posted and tracked by the team, since it impacts the manner in which the team will make decisions.

Sharing the economic information empowers team members to think of new ways to reduce costs and become more competitive. Teams are often quite innovative in reducing routine costs to free up funding for new equipment that can lead to productivity gains. However, without access to the financial information, team members are seldom committed to achieving these types of gains for their organization.

5. Quality Improvement Skills

People in an empowered work setting need to understand the common quality improvement skills. These include flow charting their work processes, cause and effect diagrams, Gantt charts, Pareto diagrams, data matrixes, and statistical tools appropriate to their work.

There are now many avenues for obtaining this training for the workforce. Community colleges, consultants, training companies, and many local Chambers of Commerce offer training concerning quality improvement skills.

6. Political Skills

All organizations have political systems in which people work, so people need to learn how to effectively plan and work within their political framework. Strategic planning and political tools, such as force field analysis, are most useful for helping teams become more politically savvy within their organization. Training materials on the basic quality tools can include information on how to prepare and use force field analysis to help a group navigate in its particular political setting.

Conclusions

How much preparation is enough to enable people to fully participate in an empowered setting? We know that pushing people into empowerment usually fails. But once people are ready, they do not want to be held back by some structured training program where someone has decided what training will be good for them. The best way to handle this problem is to focus on initial workshops or team-building that provides the concepts, then have the skill training available in modules that are available on request (just-in-time training). Explain the options and then empower the people to decide what educational help they need to be able to effectively function in the empowered work place.

John R. Dew has been a hands-on implementer of empowerment concepts and techniques for over fifteen years. This has included the development of training programs, the facilitation of teams, and leading strategic planning efforts in the private and public sectors. John currently facilitates team efforts for Lockheed

Martin Utility Services in Paducah, Kentucky, focusing on joint union and management collaboration.

John earned his doctorate in Technological and Adult Education from the University of Tennessee, writing his dissertation on educating supervisors to become team leaders.

7

Empowering for Strategic Change: 5 Fundamentals

by Steven A. Leth, Ph.D.

"Empowerment ?!?....So is that something like the kids protesting on campus and trying to take over the university administration?" I could tell from the reaction that I had just pushed the envelope and confused the middle manager with another jargon term. It was 1982 and his organization was undergoing a project designed to analyze and improve the "quality of work life." Like many management concepts before it, and many more to come, empowerment had not yet reached a general level of usage and acceptance; the concept, let alone the word, appeared to be the preoccupation of consultants and Human Resources departments. Most managers were still trying to get comfortable with employee input and feedback.

Now, fifteen years later, much has changed. Common use of the term, the availability of related "tools," many documented best practices, and, yes, many more experienced consultants attest to the acceptance and value of the concept. Most major corporations—especially the Fortune 500—with several billion in revenues have considerable experience with empowerment in business units, if not corporate-wide. In many organizations, employee empowerment was integral to their Total Quality Management efforts and presumed in any bid for the Malcolm Baldrige National Quality Award. Such stories are documented elsewhere in this publication and offer promising cases in point. But despite the general acceptance and the documentation, the real value of empowerment is not as widely appreciated as we might expect.

While most Fortune 500 firms may be experienced with empowerment, the majority of our workforce is employed in the thousands of medium and small organizations with limited resources and often less appreciation for the concept of empowerment. And even many of the major corporations that have undertaken to develop an empowered workforce have recently downsized, reengineered and restructured themselves. The remaining employees often find themselves in new circumstances with working conditions that diminish their empowerment. Indeed, recent surveys reveal that those left on the job have stress levels as high as those terminated. For much of Corporate America, empowerment is in need of renewal and revision if it is to become an integral component of business strategy and management of change.

The Challenge of Empowerment

The path to empowerment is frequently limited by weak assumptions. Often the effort has been approached much as any "program" would be with catchy slogans, speeches by senior managers, tools and techniques, and, perhaps, a "point program" for rewarding suggestions. While those provisions have value, a meaningful change in habits and beliefs will rarely follow from a short-term program quickly delegated to harried middle managers and viewed as an add-on to employee and manager responsibilities. Indeed, when viewed from the perspective of the managers and employees, empowerment often appears to be more risk than reward. Considering the experience of the middle manager, the manager's resistance is understandable in view of:

- accountability for results and deadlines; rare is the reprieve for empowerment activities, especially in the wake of recent downsizing
- "ownership" of existing practices and procedures which will be the focus of critique and change
- the prospect of fielding naive suggestions and unproductive

attempts to "reinvent the wheel"
- loss of control after working hard to finally reach a position of influence, and, importantly,
- programs chronically come and go with a lot of "hoopla," extra work and little to show for them!

Altogether, it is a perspective which hardly leads to a motivated, enthusiastic reception, and, when coupled with the concerns and doubts of some employees, the effort is in jeopardy. While many employees are eager to participate in decisions influencing their work-a-day lives, even their contribution to the effort is diminished by:

- vagueness as to what is actually expected from empowerment; signals are often mixed between giving opportunities to the employee and getting business needs met
- limited perspective and information as to what will make a difference and be a worthwhile focus
- uncertainty as to how to approach the challenge of improvement and change, even with "tools" in hand
- doubt that the extra effort will be recognized and rewarded in worthwhile ways, and, frequently,
- suspicion that the manager/supervisor is not genuinely receptive to the change imposed on the working relationship.

Progress Toward the Challenge

Looking back over several decades, perhaps the entire period since WWII, numerous corporations appear to have progressed through various stages along a path toward empowerment. And while the path is uneven and inconsistent, there seems to be a general progression from an outdated norm of "just do your job and don't ask" to a healthy, productive condition of an empowered workforce. Historically, the progression looks something like this:

FROM

- input and comments allowed and responded to by the manager or supervisor, e.g., an open door policy
- suggestions and ideas invited and perhaps rewarded financially or otherwise, e.g., suggestion systems
- improvements/changes in job procedures allowed or even encouraged, e.g., employee involvement
- assignments to undertake specific systemic or process improvements, e.g., quality or productivity efforts, and,
- collaborative roles in pursuit of strategic leverage development of core competencies and the business vision.

TO

Examples are few in number to illustrate the fifth stage; empowerment efforts that appear to be more advanced can be found in AT&T Universal Card Services, Harris Corporation, Saturn, 3M and Texas Instruments among others. But, most organizations are struggling to cope with the forces of change and to redirect their efforts from the reengineering and restructuring initiatives of the recent past. While employee participation is familiar in analytic and problem-solving activities designed to "fix" what is already in place, we have less experience with creativity and innovation applied to the development of new and unique capabilities or outputs. In the advanced stage of employee empowerment, the workforce is actively engaged in: the development of greater and new capabilities; exploring and advancing customer relationships; developing "go to market" strategies; leveraging key processes and core competencies; and implementing tactics for cultural change. In these activities, the real value of "intellectual capital" is realized; operating experience, technological expertise, marketplace savvy, and business vision are vital.

5 Fundamentals of Empowerment

For empowerment to be instrumental to strategic change, a strong foundation is built on informed perspectives, collaborative relationships and a capability to change. While not entirely "soft" issues, these do speak to understanding, motivation and knowledge. Five basic "best practices"—readily observable in organizations that have an empowerment track record—are critical to a solid foundation for empowerment. Each is followed by illustrative points.

Fundamental #1 - Empowerment is defined in the long term business plan as a strategy for change, development and growth

At the senior levels of the corporation and the business units, the "how" and "to what ends" of empowerment are outlined and clarified. Expectations for the impact on strategic initiatives, change activities, and the business vision are forthcoming. That translation and subsequent dialogues with managers and employees establishes the priority, provides focus and promotes a healthy dialogue. More than the usual amount of information about the company is needed if the expectations are to be met.

Senior managers should plan for pivotal issues and discussion of:
- where the business is headed - vision, objectives, competencies, leverage and financial targets
- how the business operates - the model/design, core processes, and critical decisions
- where employee skills and talents are needed - outcomes, capabilities, and developments
- how the daily responsibilities and routines will be affected - workload, outputs, and schedule
- how senior managers will lead empowerment - active, vocal sponsorship and example-setting.

Discussion and clarification of these issues will serve the front-end of the empowerment effort and will need to be revisited periodically for the indefinite future.

Fundamental #2 - Training encompasses tools, skills and, especially, processes for planning, supporting and implementing significant change

Both managers and employees require training in data collection and analysis techniques, problem-solving methods and, even more important, processes for change. Further, managers and supervisors should have coaching or training in how to support empowerment and innovation.

Issues for senior managers include:
- middle managers skilled at supporting and coaching employees in change activities - active listening, inspiring, collaborative problem-solving, coaching, and removing barriers
- processes or methods for planning, introducing and implementing change - gap or opportunity analysis, readiness assessments, awareness building, team development, change tactics, process design and performance measurement
- tool and skill training aligned with strategic change - tools to challenge the status quo and to create alternatives, means to identify innovative ideas, ways to address resistance, and skills in facilitating "ownership" and "buy-in."

Fundamental #3 - Managers and employees collaborate to bring about advancements, new capabilities and change in the culture

Collaboration avoids the pitfall of "delegated empowerment." In the latter, employees are "set free" to see what they come up with; it's not a scenario where talent and intellect is marshalled for strategic impact. By working together in a partnership, managers and employees are better able to align with the strategy and make a difference.

For the senior managers, related issues are:
- middle managers focused on change and strategic development - active role on teams and initiatives, working issues across boundaries, communicating feedback upward and down, and resolving impediments and turf obstacles
- implementation aligned with business strategy and vision-

progress linked to business needs, translation of changes into business leverage, and implementation lessons documented.

Fundamental #4 - Human resource and management systems reinforce and reward the empowerment practices

Active, successful empowerment is in many ways self-reinforcing; both managers and employees derive satisfaction from making a noteworthy contribution to the future of the organization and from working together along the way. However, the practices also easily diminish in the context of a heavy work schedule, and the organization should reward behavior and judgment that is critical to its future.

Senior managers should consider:
- formal endorsement and rewards for middle managers and employee efforts - public recognition of the successful empowered efforts, coaching and performance appraisal that emphasizes empowerment, behavior requisite for advancement, and linkages to bonuses and salary increases
- features of the selection and development processes - criteria in the hiring process (experience and behaviors), core curricula for training, and a consideration in cross-training and mentoring.

Fundamental # 5 - Business accomplishments and results impacted by the empowerment effort are celebrated and communicated across the organization

Corporate communication is often devoted to updates and reviews of operations and frequently lacks substance. Empowerment focused on significant business objectives warrants open discussion and in-depth coverage. Employees engaged in changing the conduct of business are making a major contribution; communication about that contribution should offer substance and avoid a gratuitous approach. Further, recognition and celebration of the accomplishments places an emphasis on the results of empowerment and not merely the process or activities.

Issues for the senior managers include:
- communication media used to promote empowerment as a key to strategic change - outlining and clarifying the business strategy, describing executive expectations, and overviewing empowerment tactics
- documented and communicated results and outcomes - real accomplishments, lessons learned, and business results
- success celebrated and contributions acknowledged - events to celebrate achievements, credit to whom it is due, and rewards distributed.

Conclusion

A revisit to that middle manager would be interesting. His corporation has undergone significant change in an industry (steel) that's been characterized by upheaval and decades of fierce international competition. If ever an empowered workforce could make a difference, it is in those embattled industries where the value of every major resource should be fully realized.

The "intellectual capital" that resides in the workforce is not limited to specialized functions like research and development, marketing or strategic planning. Employees who are well-informed about the business, trained in the strategies and tactics of change, engaged in initiatives to leverage competencies, and rewarded for making real contributions are key to strategic change. Rather than merely allowing these conditions to eventually emerge, senior managers are challenged to provide a solid foundation and incorporate empowerment in the strategy for change.

Steven A. Leth is President of The Institute, a Houston, Texas-based resource for strategic change and development. He developed the Service Quality Management and Business Process Reengineering services for The Institute and has delivered related consulting and training support to a variety of clients. Steve has consulted to more than 60 corporations and agencies spanning seven major industry groups: aerospace/defense, communications, business services, consumer products, energy, petrochemicals and healthcare.

Earlier, as senior vice president with the American Productivity & Quality Center, he developed the Center's strategic thrust in functional redesign and service-related improvement, a comprehensive process/method that has been used by several hundred organizations. Steve holds a doctorate in organizational communication and industrial administration from Purdue University, is published, and is an adjunct faculty member at Rice University.

8

Determining Your Employee Involvement and Empowerment Strategy

by John N. Younker, Ph.D.

In recent years, more and more business organizations have elected to adopt some form of employee involvement and empowerment. Many of these companies were hoping to enhance their customer service images; to be viewed as being "service oriented." The use of empowerment has taken on an almost religious-like zeal. Unfortunately, far too many organizations selected approaches to employee involvement and empowerment that are not suited to their specific business conditions and operations. They failed to create an optimum fit—an appropriate match between their organization's needs and an approach to employee involvement and empowerment that is best suited to meet those needs.

Numerous articles and book chapters have been written about empowerment and the impact that "turning the front-line employees loose" has had on improving service. Companies such as Scandinavian Airlines (SAS), Marriott Hotels, AT&T Universal Card, and Federal Express have all been touted as having empowered employees who are utilizing creativity and innovation in serving their customers. Workers in these organizations are being asked to participate in the development of new services and products, manage key customer interfaces, and creatively solve operational problems.

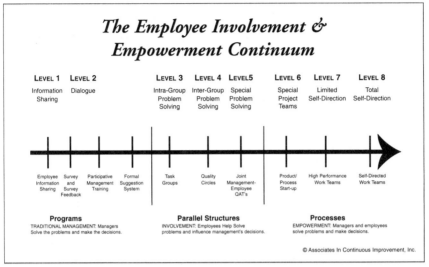

Figure 1

The Choices

There are several approaches to employee involvement and empowerment for senior managers to select from. Figure 1 is a "continuum" of approaches to employee involvement and empowerment. As you increase in the level of empowerment, the degree of autonomy in decision making is significantly increased.

The choice of which approach to use is a function of the degree to which senior management provides its employees with:

- Access to critical business information (e.g. operating results, performance of competitors, customer requirements, etc.)
- Training to effectively use the information and perform (e.g. problem solving skills, planning skills, etc.)
- Authority and discretion to take prompt and appropriate action (e.g. resolution of customer issues and concerns, work process redesign, etc.)
- Opportunities to make valuable contributions and key decisions (e.g. quality circles, project teams, self-directed work teams, etc.)
- Recognition and rewards for accepting and exercising the

responsibility necessary to get their jobs done, as well as assisting others in doing their jobs (e.g. pay-for-performance, gainsharing, etc.).

All of these factors need to be addressed by senior management in the development of an employee involvement and empowerment strategy.

Benefits and Costs

Extensive field research has been conducted on the use of employee involvement and empowerment in the work setting by such organizations as the American Productivity & Quality Center, the Center for Effective Organizations, the Center for Creative Leadership, the U.S. General Accounting Office and the Quality & Productivity Management Association. The documented potential benefits of employee involvement and empowerment are:

- Higher levels of product and service quality
- Increased levels of performance and productivity
- More rapid response to customer requests
- Quicker response to customer concerns and/or complaints
- Enhanced levels of customer retention and praise
- Greater attraction and retention of higher performing employees
- Higher levels of employee self-esteem
- Increased levels of employee innovation and creativity
- More effective problem solving and decision making
- Greater levels of job knowledge and skills
- Enhanced staffing flexibility
- More self-management capability and reduced need for traditional supervision.

Of course, these benefits do not come without a price. The same field research that identified the benefits of employee involvement and empowerment also documented the potential costs. They are:

- Higher employee selection, training, and compensation costs
- Increased employee expectations for growth and development and overall organizational change
- Increased levels of middle manager and first-line supervisor dissatisfaction and resistance to change
- Increased need for support systems and structures
- *Instances* of slower and/or inconsistent customer service
- Perceived violations of equity and fair play
- Some bad decisions and giveaways
- Dissatisfaction and resistance to change by support staff
- Employee anxiety and resistance to change.

By knowing both the benefits and costs, the decision to use a particular approach to employee involvement and empowerment can be made because it is the appropriate response to the organization's situation and specific needs, not just because it is what everyone else is doing.

Assessment & Analysis

As is shown on the Figure 1 continuum, there are three distinct approaches to employee involvement and empowerment; programs, parallel systems and processes. These approaches represent increasing levels of employee involvement and empowerment as additional access to business information, training, authority, decision-making opportunities, and recognition and rewards are provided to the front-line employees. Therefore, the approach to employee involvement and empowerment that senior management must choose is a complex decision. Rather than being a simple, either/or alternative, it is a decision that requires consideration of what is best suited for the organization, the employees, and the business conditions.

Research conducted by David Bowen and Edward Lawler has resulted in the development of organizational contingencies upon which senior management should base their employee involvement and empowerment strategies. These contingencies are five situational factors that will have a major impact upon the fit of the selected approach to employee involvement and empowerment. They are:

- *Basic Business Strategy* - the degree to which an organization desires to be seen in their market segment as the benchmark in quality and customer responsiveness. The willingness of a company to provide personalized service with a lot of TLC. Two examples of companies who have a basic business strategy that are strongly based on these factors are L.L. Bean and Club Med
- *Relationship With Customers* - the degree to which having an enduring relationship with your customers is a critical part of your overall service package. Two examples of companies that have such relationships with their customers are The Marriott Hotels and Conference Centers and USAA
- *Technology* - the degree to which an organization's job content (technology) is complex and challenging. Two examples of organizations that have challenging and complex technologies are Amdahl and AMP
- *Business Environment* - the degree to which an organization does not require routine procedures, high-control management practices, and predictable markets in order to be successful. Two examples of organizations that have been highly successful in this type of business environment are SAS and Federal Express
- *Types of Managers and Employees* - the degree to which an organization's managers and employees have a need to grow and to be challenged, where there exists a sense of "common fate" and unity. Two examples of organizations that are staffed by these type of managers and employees are Saturn and Nordstrom.

Senior managers need to conduct an assessment and analysis of their companies in relation to the five contingencies.

To assist senior managers in this assessment and analysis the "Employee Involvement & Empowerment Questionnaire" was developed (see Figure 2). This simple, straightforward questionnaire can be used by senior mangers to rate their organizations against each of the five contingencies discussed above. The questionnaire utilizes a 1 - 5 Likert Ranking Scale to determine the degree of fit between their overall organizational situation and the alternative approaches to employee involvement and empowerment. The following propositions suggest how to match the organizational situations with the possible approaches.

- Proposition 1: The higher the rating on each contingency, the better the fit with an employee involvement and empowerment approach.
- Proposition 2: The total score on all five contingencies will help pinpoint the fit with the appropriate approach to employee involvement and empowerment, as follows: Programs (5 - 10 pts.) Parallel Systems (10 - 20 pts.) Processes (21 - 25 pts.).
- Proposition 3: The higher the total score, the more the benefits of increasing the level of employee involvement and empowerment will outweigh the costs.

Employee Involvement & Empowerment Contingency Questionnaire

Instructions: Select and circle the ranking that best fits your organization's situation in each of the five contingencies.

Contingency	Low Level EI&E	High Level EI&E

Basic Business Strategy:
 (high volume/low cost) (personalized/customized/differentiated)
  1   2   3   4   5

Relationship With Customers:
 (transaction oriented/short term) (relationship oriented/long term)
  1   2   3   4   5

Technology:
 (routine process/low tech) (non routine/complex/high tech)
  1   2   3   4   5

Business Environment:
 (predictable/few surprises) (unpredictable/many surprises)
  1   2   3   4   5

Types of Managers and Employees:
 (Managers - Theory X) (Managers - Theory Y)
 (Employees - low growth needs, low social needs, weak interpersonal skills) (Employees - high growth needs, high social needs, strong interpersonal skills)
  1   2   3   4   5

Figure 2

After each member of senior management has had an opportunity to complete this questionnaire, the results should be shared and discussed by them in an effort to reach a consensus on their organization's current situation and then decide on the best fit (approach) to employee involvement and empowerment for their organization.

Some questions that can be used to guide this discussion are:
- Given our company's mission and our product/service focus, what would be the value added from spending the necessary dollars on employee selection, training, and retention that would be required by an employee involvement and empowerment effort?
- Would our customers be willing to pay for some or all of the costs of these efforts?
- Do we know and fully understand our customers' needs and service requirements?
- Would an approach to employee involvement and empowerment that results in high levels of employee autonomy and TLC work best in our market segment, or is speed, low cost, and predictability more important to our customers?
- Does our service delivery also include managing the relationships with our customers or is it a simple transaction?
- Are our relationships with our customers the primary commodity we offer; is this our market niche/differentiation?
- Is our company's technology so simple and straightforward that we would be better off doing a better job with our old management practices?
- Is our business environment predictable or unpredictable?
- Do we have the right type of managers and employees to support a high involvement and empowerment culture?

In closing, it is important that we recognize that the level of global competition is increasing and that this will result in further demands by our customers to be more responsive to their needs and requirements. This, in turn, will lead to more pressure on senior management to implement employee involvement and empowerment practices in their companies. It is at this point that they need to determine the best approach to employee involvement and empowerment for their organization's needs and current business situation.

John N. Younker is the President and co-founder of Associates In Continuous Improvement, in Houston, Texas. His focus includes the coaching of CEOs and executive managers, visioning and direction-setting/strategic performance planning, organizational transition and change, and executive management team building. He has consulted to a broad range of industries including construction, real estate development, defense, engineering, healthcare, insurance, paper and wood products, petrochemicals, telecommunications, transportation, and public utilities.

Earlier, as a vice president at the American Productivity & Quality Center, he was extensively involved in research and advisory initiatives that focused on employee involvement and empowerment, the development of high performing work teams, organization assessment and planning, and service quality improvement. John holds a doctorate in industrial-organizational psychology from The University of Memphis, is published, and is an adjunct professor at two universities.

Part Three

Deploying and Managing Empowerment— 6 Case Studies

"Managers do not motivate employees by giving them higher wages, more benefits, or new status symbols. Rather, employees are motivated by their own inherent need to succeed at a challenging task. The manager's job, then, is not to motivate people to get them to achieve; instead the manager should provide opportunities for people so they will become motivated."

—Frederick Herzberg

9

Managing Empowerment at Marriott

For the first 40 or 50 years of its existence, the Marriott hotel chain enjoyed annual growth of at least 20%. Then a few years ago, the bottom suddenly fell out of the economy. Clearly, Marriott had to do something to maintain its momentum. Corporate headquarters in Washington, D.C. decided the answer was a quality improvement effort.

Today, as a result of TQM, associates at the Atlanta Marriott Marquis are being empowered on every level to be decision-makers. Marquis managers recently told how they're managing empowerment. They talked about moving from traditional management to empowerment, about their empowerment structure, TQM training, boundaries, results, what empowerment feels like to supervisors, and where empowerment is headed at the Marquis.

Opened in 1985, the Atlanta Marriott Marquis is primarily a convention hotel and the second largest in the Marriott chain, with 1,674 rooms and 1,300 associates.

From Traditional Management to Empowerment

"Because of empowerment, traditional management is becoming a thing of the past here," said Nancy Curtin, director of TQM/training.

"Today about 20 percent of our management is traditional, 30 percent is empowering, and 50 percent is involving but moving in the right direction. Some traditional managers find this to be an uncomfortable environment and choose not to stay.

"When you consider that our Marquis Executive Committee had always been given directives from the top level, and that now hourly associates are being involved in making decisions, we've come a long way.

"In theory, TQM at Marriott is a corporate-driven program. In actuality, it is a hotel-driven process because each hotel does its own things, though we have a common mission. To our General Manager, Ted Renner, who opened the hotel seven years ago, TQM was perfect for us."

One of the hotel's first steps was to form 135 Quality Action Teams of 10 associates each, involving everyone. (They started as problem-solving groups, but are becoming a key mechanism for empowerment.) Except for a few hourly associates, the team leaders were managers or supervisors.

"At first, the teams were very top-down driven," explained Curtin. "But they began saying, 'We don't have a lot we're working on right now, so we'll meet once a month.'

"To a degree, that's real empowerment because, before, they had been told, 'You will meet once a week.' Then they would get together and not know what to do. Now they're deciding when they'll meet and what they'll work on. So, they've come a long way. Our goal is to have self-managed teams, but we're not there yet."

The hotel initiated Q-Tips, a system that encourages associates to suggest improvement ideas. Individuals simply fill out a form and drop it in a Q-Tips box. The Hotel Steering Committee decides what ideas have merit. Plans are to have a Q-Tips hotline to make the system easier to use.

The Empowerment Structure

The Marquis' empowerment structure includes: Quality Action Teams (already mentioned); they involve all hourly associates in developing and implementing improvement projects. In the first year alone, Q-Tips and Quality Action Teams generated more than 2,400 ideas, about 90% of which were implemented. In the preceding year, only 12 ideas had been suggested.

Department Steering Committees: Each of the hotel's 23 departments has a Department Steering Committee comprised of team leaders. The committee overseas the Quality Action Teams within its department.

Hotel Steering Committee: One representative from each department sits on this committee, which is the highest governing body in the hotel's quality process. The committee meets bi-weekly to discuss total hotel issues.

Quality Improvement Team: This team wrote the Marquis' vision statement and created the Quality Action Team concept. It has ten members, including the general manager, director of training, two Marquis Executive Committee members, selected managers from a cross-section of the hotel, and two associates.

"As members leave, we plan to add more associates, so that eventually half the members will be hourly associates," said Curtin.

The Quality Improvement Team is the liaison between the Hotel Steering Committee and those in the regional and corporate offices who are guiding Marriott's overall quality improvement effort. It also organizes and plans how to roll out the TQM process within the Hotel.

"This is the 'think tank' group, and the Hotel Steering Committee is the 'make it happen' group," explained Curtin.

Training a Key First Step

"Our Quality Action Team leaders went through 14 hours of training in one month," explained Curtin. "Their classes included everything from introduction to Deming, to process management and how to run meetings and keep records."

Corporate headquarters brought in outside consultants, provided materials and also trained key people like Curtin and TQM Manager, Don Geiger.

As of this writing, the associates have gone through two courses: TQM1, Empowerment; and TQM2, Problem-Solving Tools. TQM3 will focus on Group Process and Using Tools in a Team Environment, and TQM4 and TQM5 will be either Benchmarking or Tracking and Measuring.

"The TQM training varied from four to eight hours and was cascaded, starting with J. W. Marriott, Jr. and his direct reports," explained Curtin. "Our hotel's empowerment training was not all that effective, however. Different people taught it and the course became their interpretation of empowerment.

"When we conducted TQM2 at this hotel, a lot of the empowerment issues finally came out. TQM2 provided the associates an opportunity to talk to each other and their managers."

TQM2 was conducted first in a 3-day event with 200 supervisors, 100 managers and 200 hourly associates who were either key players or the biggest dissenters about TQM. The latter were included to try to "bring them around."

Explained Curtin, "The course included a Customer Forum in which three customers talked about what the Marquis is doing right, or wrong. We also conducted an Executive Committee Forum to give associates an opportunity to speak with the executives, which isn't often possible in a hotel this size.

"And we included a Quality Team Forum in which two teams that were doing well and two that were not doing so well answered questions from associates.

"The main event was the Executive Committee's presentation of the hotel's game plan for the year, with the associates giving feedback. The committee talked about revenue sharing, cash conservation, associate satisfaction and customer satisfaction. Changes in the game plan were made, based on the associates' comments. The associates voted on proposed changes and the majority decided.

"If for any legal or monetary reasons the Executive Committee couldn't make a change, they were required to explain why. The game plan was again presented the next day, with the revisions in bold type. This process was empowered behavior and it was also involvement in writing the game plan.

"We followed up this training with two one-day training events to start the remaining 800 associates on the process. Don and I facilitated this training, which was a consolidation of the three-day event because the first 500 who were trained were already working on the process with the 800."

TQM3 is a two-part course: the first, a course in group dynamics; the second involving control charts to measure results.

"We don't have TQM3 rolled out yet," said Geiger. "When we do, I think we'll see our greatest leaps forward because people will start to focus on their processes.

"The control chart may be difficult for some associates to understand, but the associates won't have difficulty seeing that they're working within the control limits."

Establishing Boundaries

During the initial training, department managers and associates set boundaries so that associates would know what they were empowered or not empowered to do. Now, all 23 departments of the hotel have associates' empowerment boundaries written and posted.

Explained Geiger, "They went through exercises in which they were asked, 'What's your low risk, your high risk, your safe zone?' Then they decided where in the low risk they could put boundaries. They avoided high risk areas."

Explained Curtin, "Some boundaries are minor, but to the associate, they're a big deal. For example, being able to give a movie rebate of $7.95 to a guest who said he fell asleep and didn't watch the movie.

"Or, being able to give away amenities. People often say, 'I really like your hand cream. May I have a few bottles?' Before there were boundaries, a housekeeper would have to call a manager. Now she's empowered to take care of her customer.

"Our empowerment training was entitled, 'Whatever It Takes.' We tried to teach the associates that they're empowered to do whatever it takes to satisfy our guests. They're even empowered to leave their work areas to help a guest.

"In a hotel this size, guests often can't find their way round. Before we had boundaries, associates would try to give directions. Now they're empowered to leave their work stations and take guests to their destination without getting into trouble for doing it.

"Another beneficial thing we did," continued Curtin, " was to differentiate between empowerment and heroics. We'll do whatever it takes to satisfy a guest, but we've got to be reasonable and within the law. For example, associates in our lounges are not empowered to serve alcohol after the hours the State says they can.

"Before this, if you were to ask associates what their boundaries were, they wouldn't have known. I, personally, felt uncomfortable doing something outside of my department. For example, if a guest had a complaint about one of our restaurants, I would have said, 'That's too bad.' Now, I'll step in and see how I can satisfy the guest.

"We've added a third day to our orientation to review with new associates the boundaries for their department."

Added Geiger, "We've found that reinforcement is needed to remember boundaries. Some associates may not know exactly what the dollar limits of their boundaries are. But they know instinctively what they're empowered to do. And some learn by modeling what other associates do."

"The front desk has tiered their boundaries," said Curtin. "They've modeled them after our Honored Guest Program, with Gold, Black and Platinum levels, each with specific boundaries [See box, next page.]

"When this was begun, the associates started at Gold, no matter how experienced they were. They can be elevated to the next level by making a request to their manager and then being assessed by a group of team leaders.

"Other departments are also considering having levels of boundaries. The boundaries are also reviewed from time to time."

Empowerment Boundaries — Front Desk Associates

Gold	Platinum
• Apologize. • Room move. • Turndown service. • Rebate movie. • Rebate phone call. • Advise manager when leaving desk to resolve. • Guest problem time allowed will be set. • Take action. • Follow-up (Guest Services).	• Apologize. • Room move. • Turndown service. • Rebate movie. • Rebate phone call. • Advise manager when leaving desk to resolve. • Guest problem time allowed will be set. • Take action. • Amenity up to $25 value. • Breakfast/Parking. • Problem or service up to $500. • Incorrect rate adjustments/as much as needed. • Override selling strategy. • Authorize associates schedule switches (flip flop initial approval). • Close and verify shift closings and drops.
Black	
• Apologize. • Room move. • Turndown service. • Rebate movie. • Rebate phone call. • Advise manager when leaving desk to resolve. • Guest problem time allowed will be set. • Take action. • Follow-up (Guest Services). • Amenity up to $45 value. • Breakfast/Parking. • Rebate or offer service value up to $200. • Incorrect rate adjustment up to $600. • Take off disputed charge up to $100 without outlet approval (all charges need backup).	
	All
	• No complimentary rooms (must be rebate). • Cannot override selling strategy (except platinum level.) • No schedule changes without a manager's approval. • No selling presidential suites. • No overriding another associate in front of a guest. • Maintain hotel rules/stay within the law.

Housekeeping Cleans Up

"We're always looking for ways to reduce inventory and increase cash flow," said Geiger. "A supervisor in housekeeping initiated a project to track the linens in king rooms to see if we could reduce the amount without negatively affecting the guests.

"For three months, an Action Team tracked the king rooms on 15 floors and concluded that all the towels were not being used. Then, on a small scale, they reduced the number of towels in king rooms on six floors. In just three months, there were very few requests from guests for more linen, and the reduction saved the hotel about $5,000."

Another example was recalled by Kent Florence, houseman supervisor. "A team in housekeeping initiated the 'perfect room' project," he said. "Using a fishbone diagram, they determined that to achieve the perfect room, they needed enough linens on the floor, fewer rooms to clean, enough supplies, teamwork, less pressure from supervisors and a better attitude about ASAP rooms."

In response to the team's findings, the hotel added a second laundry shift. They also are experimenting by assigning some housekeepers fewer rooms to clean. If it proves successful, the policy will be adopted throughout the hotel.

What Empowerment Feels Like to Supervisors

Shanda Blake, engineering supervisor, has been with Marriott 11 years. Empowerment to her is "my peers and my managers telling me that I can make decisions and help the hotel. It also means making decisions without being disciplined if they're not good decisions. If I make a mistake, I don't get a slap on the hand. I learn from the mistake and go on.

"If my supervisor isn't here, I can fill in for him because my training has prepared me. And I feel good about it. That's empowerment.

"We still have barriers," she continued. "But Marriott is telling me I count and my opinion counts. They wouldn't have spent time and money to train me if they didn't want me to apply what I've learned. It's not always pleasant to challenge the barriers. But if you care enough, you'll get past them. If you talk to enough people, someone is going to listen."

Said Robert Bennett, floor maintenance supervisor, "The associates feel more motivated and, quite naturally, motivated associates give you better work. That's what it's all about—satisfaction for the associates, which is satisfaction for the management, and satisfaction for the guests, our main function. If the guests are satisfied, they're going to come back.

"The associates are satisfied because they have a say, they have empowerment and they have boundaries so they can take care of the guests' requests faster. They don't have to say, 'Wait until I ask my manager'—who needs to ask his supervisor. The associate can act on the spot."

Said Reginald Brown, front desk supervisor, "Having boundaries shows me where I am as an individual in this company, what I'm able to do and what my associates are able to do as far as decisions are concerned. We can clear things up without worrying about repercussions.

"It frees me to handle other situations and be more interactive with other associates and guests. Having boundaries spreads out the decisions. The concept makes everyone feel equally important. Most associates love being empowered. They feel in control of a situation, and the customer feels better."

Where It's Headed

"We can't do business in the 90s the same way we've been doing it in the past," said Ted Renner, general manager. "In a global, more competitive economy, there must be a better way to manage business.

"In the past, we've been top-driven and the typical workers were followers. There was a teacher-student or parent-child relationship. Today, we've got to change the mentality and ask managers to be coaches. The coach of a professional team doesn't go out on the field and run the team. He coaches and the players do their best.

"We get better results if everyone at all levels becomes a leader and plays a vital part in day-to-day business activities.

"This movement of empowerment is different from programs or initiatives. It's a movement to bring about a cultural change. Today we're setting the foundation. Much like in building construction, you need blueprints, direction, vision. A lot of effort is expended assembling players, having objectives and providing training. But this is all below ground level and not seen.

"Some people want to see results today. But you can't build a 100-story building in one day. I hope that in five years, everyone at every layer of this hotel will have the ability to make decisions, bring about change, serve the needs of the customers and provide the ultimate in hospitality and service.

"My job is to create the atmosphere that will allow ideas to surface and bring about change to improve service to guests. I need to provide everyone with the same information and experiences so they can have security and confidence in their decision-making ability.

"I also need to be the leader in making the vision happen and yet not dominate, as under the old culture. I need to be a total resource and also commit the time and financial resources to TQM and not say the budget won't allow it.

"As more people are involved in decisions, fewer managers are needed. The Marquis had 127 managers and now has 95, with a goal to reach 50. No manager has lost his or her job, but has been given new responsibilities. We're looking for ways to reduce management; so when there is attrition, we ask, 'Is this a role that can be absorbed?'

"For example, Marriott abolished its Guest Relations (complaint) Department because the guests are now being served in every area of the hotel at the moment of truth, with an associate interacting with a guest. That's where it's got to happen.

"We're seeing the results of our Quality Improvement Process and empowerment. Today, we have the highest market share and occupancy rate in our area. But we're not taking from the other hotels' share of the pie—we're expanding the pie so there's more for everyone.

"Empowerment is the way to set yourself apart from the competition."

Date of Case Study: August, 1992

1997 Epilogue: "Our TQM effort has continued to evolve during the past four years, and empowerment has progressed quite nicely," said Ted Renner in December 1996. "We continue to have the highest market share in the area's hotel community. We've had good revenue increases and cost savings, and guest satisfaction indicators have continued to grow—as have guest comments about individual associates.

"TQM is no longer a separate program. It's not something we do only when we've accomplished the rest of our business. It's the way we perform day in and day out. Things have evolved to where the department heads are responsible for creating the right environment, for challenging people, for listening and for implementing improvements. When associates surface ideas that can't be dealt with at the department level, they're brought to the Quality Improvement Council. We're continuing to try self-managed teams, but we've found that many people still aren't ready for them and that there may not be a need for them where everybody shares in empowerment.

"The concept of empowerment has been firmly adopted here. Based on surveys we've done, everyone prefers to operate in this way and no one wants to change it. The empowerment boundaries haven't changed significantly since they were established; I believe that's an indication of the sound thinking we did in setting them up. In a recent anonymous opinion survey of associates, 82% said they feel confident to make decisions or take actions to satisfy our guests, and 83% said they are involved in improving how work is done and how guests are served. We believe the remaining people are not understanding or embracing the concept or are new to the hotel and not used to the idea yet.

"I'm retiring this month and the new general manager was the GM of our San Antonio River Center property where these same things have been done very successfully. I'm confident that he'll carry on."

10

Training for Empowerment at Martin Marietta Energy Systems

For many years, the facilities currently managed by Martin Marietta Energy Systems (MMES) for the U.S. Department of Energy were among the only suppliers of enriched uranium for nuclear power plants and of very specialized high-precision machining capabilities used in the United States defense program. Today, however, with the fall of the Berlin Wall and the end of the Cold War, the situation has changed dramatically.

Now, other companies and other countries are moving into these markets, and, for the first time in the nearly 50-year history of the Oak Ridge, Tennessee plants, employees are having to deal with how to survive with competition. A key strategy for responding to this sudden change in business climate and maintaining world leadership in these fields is to empower people throughout the company.

The U.S. government is the primary customer for Martin Marietta Energy Systems, a subsidiary of Martin Marietta Corporation. Today, with Energy Systems President Clyde Hopkins championing empowerment, about 10 to 15% of the company's 21,000 employees at its five locations in Oak Ridge, Paducah, Kentucky, and Piketon, Ohio are working in empowered situations. And the percentage is climbing steadily.

A few of the empowered teams, some of which are cross-functional, are self-managed. Most, however, have leader-facilitators and potential to evolve into self-managed teams.

A group of MMES managers and leader-facilitators talked about a key factor that's helping them to move from traditional management to empowerment: empowerment training.

Breakthrough Divisions

"We began our empowerment training about four years ago by including one day of training on self-managed teams in our Advanced Management Program for middle managers," explained John Dew, TQM manager at one of the sites. "Our objective was to create an awareness of empowerment issues. We brought in university professors and senior managers to teach workshops.

"We wanted everyone to understand that people have been experimenting with empowerment for 40 to 50 years. Empowerment is not just a fad, or a half-baked idea some training person is trying to sell. Research shows that empowerment is a very effective way to run our organization.

"Next, we began looking for breakthrough organizations with division directors who would be willing to champion empowerment. Barbara Ashdown, director of our Information Services Division, and Donna Griffith, director of our Publications Division, were two of the managers willing to lead the way."

Their divisions are part of Information Resources and Administration (IRA) organization, headed by Dan Robbins. IRA is a white collar unit whose divisions primarily serve the MMES-managed sites in Oak Ridge.

Continued Dew, "With a focus group of leader-facilitators (former supervisors in a new role) we assessed training needs. From this information we put together a two-day workshop called Facilitating Work Teams. Now, the training for supervisors is a half day, and teams spend a half day in orientation and a whole day in skills building."

Empowerment is a Means, Not an End

"What inspired me to get started with empowerment training in Publications," recalled Griffith, "was a 1989 communications survey we conducted. The employees gave us low scores on involvement in decision making. And it looked as if they were ready to have a larger role. I think I also innately believed there was a better way to do things.

"In the beginning, if I hadn't seen major payoffs for the time and energy invested—from both organizational and personal standpoints—it would have been hard to continue. For me, the payoff was developing people.

"It's a criminal waste for people to throw away days and days of their lives between 8 a.m. and 5 p.m. and to think their real lives begin after they leave work. I wanted to find a way to tap their potential and get them excited about their work. If you can do that, the numbers will follow.

"You have to create an environment in which managers can discover what's in it for themselves," continued Griffith. "And when they have to be straight with employees. If they're not doing empowerment to develop people, they shouldn't say they are. People are going to know if the manager has another primary driver, like improving the bottom line.

"Empowerment is a means to an end, and not an end in itself. The end could be: delivering quality products to customers, or continuous improvement, or embracing values.

"A value we're trying to get across is valuing people. One way to do this is to give people some control over their destiny in the workplace. Empowerment helps them help themselves.

"But if you succeed in empowering people and the business fails, you won't feel good about yourself. To be successful, empowerment has to lead to achievement of goals that support the mission of the organization."

Sense of Common Mission

Recalling how the Information Services Division began its empowerment effort, Ashdown said, "We started with training on teaming and on the process of change. Because it helps teams to have a sense of their common mission, we agreed that they should create a charter. This included such things as developing a mission and vision and defining roles and responsibilities.

"Most teams take about a year to do the chartering. The time depends upon the working relationship already in the group. The less trust there is, the longer it takes.

"We also organized the leader-facilitators into a team. They share leadership responsibilities and have a goal to create an environment that supports personal growth.

"You have to nurture people. And you have to get a certain percentage of them—a critical mass—to buy in. Once you get used to operating this way, you don't want to operate any other way, because nothing else is effective.

"So you run up against the rest of organization still operating in the old mode. And you become a kind of change agent in every situation because you're trying to negotiate with everyone around you to take a more enlightened approach to making decisions."

Teams Have an Option

Employees are given the option to work in empowered teams, or to continue in the traditional mode. Explained middle manager Randy Hoffman, "The process is evolutionary. Part of it involves helping people become aware of empowerment. At that point, they have to decide how they want to operate.

"Their choice depends upon their division. In mine, we don't push people who are resistant to the idea. We're more interested in working with groups ready to change and who are moving in that direction."

Added middle-manager Catherine Nook, "It's not totally the team's choice, however. Teams can oust their supervisors. There has to be agreement on roles and responsibilities so that everyone works in a team environment. "

Explained middle manager David Baumgardner, "We're trying to give everybody a choice. But at the same time, we're putting a lot of energy, time and resources into our vision of empowerment. One of these days, we expect to get there. So, the implication is, if you don't go with us, ultimately you'll need to recognize that that's where we're going.

"But managers have to understand as they go into this process that they don't abdicate their role as leader. They're not just giving the work over to the people. They don't abdicate their responsibilities. They share them. They become a resource and teach, coach and counsel. But they're still a leader and provide guidance. That's probably why they had their job in the first place. So it's very important that they're an integral part of this process."

MMES continues to have some teams with traditional supervisors. Explained Dew, "The line of demarcation is whether the decision-making role has been changed so that many of the decisions are being made by the team."

"Situational" Empowerment

Continued Dew, "Empowering means establishing boundaries within which employees are going to work, and then freeing them up to run things and make decisions within those boundaries. We have a wide diversity of empowerment efforts under way at all five of our sites. There's no exact formula we follow because it becomes the antithesis of empowerment to say, 'This is the way you empower people.'

"We've got different business units and different historical backgrounds. That creates a big difference in how you go about empowering people.

"So we let each site decide how empowering can best be done in their part of the organization. That may seem a little chaotic, but a little chaos is working well for us now."

Said Audrey Byrd, TQM specialist for Publications and facilitator for the IRA Empowerment Assistance Council, "Not having a road map is at once the worst thing, and the best thing, about our empowering effort. There are no steps—one, two, three, four—and this isn't comforting to people who want them."

Added Dew, "This sometimes makes problems for people from one part of the organization who are trying to relate to another part. One group says, 'We're forming performance measurement teams. Why aren't you?' Well, that may work fine for them. But something else works well for another part of the organization. We're all headed in the same direction but taking different paths. There are many paths up the mountain."

"Situational" Training

Because of IRA's "situational" approach to empowerment, there is also a situational approach to training.

"There is no prescribed training," said Leader-Facilitator Mona Jones. "If management or the teams see the need for certain courses, they call them in."

"Our training is staged," explained Leader-Facilitator Anne Travis. "First, each team develops its mission and goals. Then they do in-depth training. They may work on group dynamics, conflict resolution or other problems. In the early stages, they don't need this kind of training because they aren't that far down the road."

Added Byrd, "We've developed a matrix to get some idea of where Publications staff members are concerning training needs. We gave them a list of typical training categories, such as Understanding Personalities, and Conflict Management. Then we asked, 'If you had some money for training, what would you spend it on first?' The matrix gives them a resource list."

The training is basically of two types [see box]: 1) traditional classroom training, with syllabus; and 2) organizational development "interventions."

IRA also recently held a workshop on empowerment for all its

> ### Empowerment Training at MMES
>
> **I. Classroom training**
> - "Advanced Management Program"
>   To help managers learn about self-managed teams and transition to role of leader-facilitator; delivered by senior managers and professors. Includes one day with Dr. Leonard Berger from Clemson University on self-managed teams.
> - "Facilitating Work Teams"
>   A two day workshop developed in-house based on input from leader-facilitators and team members. Focuses on conflict management, measurement processes, communications skills, running meetings, listening skills, and self management concepts.
> - "Managing for Excellence," "Managing Interpersonal Relationships," "Creating High-Performance Teams"
>   For all leader-facilitators and many team members; delivered by Wilson Learning Corp.
> - "The Consultative Process," "Advanced Facilitation," "Innovator"
>   For IRA staff members who become internal consultants, delivered by Wilson.
> - Kepner-Tregoe Problem Solving/Decision Making
>   Additional training for IRA Staff.
>
> **II. Organizational development "interventions"**
> Administration and interpretation of *Myers Briggs Inventory,* and facilitation of groups/issues. For teams; delivered by Pat Green Associates.
>
> **III. Classroom training**
> An open forum and three workshops:
> 1. *"Conflict Management"*
>   For Empowerment Assistance
> 2. *"Leadership for Managers"*
>   For Managers.
> 3. *"Negotiation"*
>   For team members.

staff, which was a combination of both types of training.

Long-term Improvement

Some teams rely heavily on personality assessment. "We have three approaches to personality profiles," explained Dew, "Myers-Briggs Inventory, Wilson Learning's Managing Interpersonal Relations, and I Speak Your Language.

"One of our teams was made up of people who had experienced a lot of interpersonal conflict. When it was first suggested that they be formed into a self-managed team, the idea was extremely controversial. We had to bring in a consultant to help them work through their differences.

"They also believed they couldn't work as a self-managed team because of administrative barriers in their work area. We were able to remove the barriers, so now they're a self-managed team that's taking on tremendous responsibilities. They've learned to work with each other, and they're an award-winning team.

"Some people might say we're getting short-term higher levels of performance because we provided more attention to this team. But actually, we're getting long-term improved performance because we were willing to train them."

Reenforcing Empowerment

To support the empowerment effort, Dan Robbins, director of IRA, established the Empowerment Assistance Council, which provides training resources and internal consultants who are experienced in empowering and are trained to help less-experienced teams. The council is comprised of about 18 members, including Robbins, the division directors, middle and line managers and team members.

"Another way we increased empowerment in Publications," said Leader-Facilitator Carolyn Moser, "was to establish a Division Council and also a Site Council at each of the three sites. These focus on employee issues and help manage the division."

"It would be a mistake to assume empowerment isn't threatening to people," said Mona Jones. "At first, there was a lot of mistrust. Everyone thought the empowerment effort was something that would be gone, and there would be something new next year. There still are some very traditional managers in our organization.

"But empowerment is supported by super division directors, who are champions. Now we're involved in things we've never been involved in before, such as the budget. We have more information than we could ever have hoped for."

Effectiveness of Training

Said Anne Travis, "On a scale of one to five, I'd say the training was a five. I'm sorry we didn't have it five years ago when my team was formed. Some rough and rocky places would have been a lot smoother."

Added Sandy Holt, leader-facilitator, "In my work group, the feedback was negative at first. People said, 'This can't possibly work.' But the training demonstrated how barriers could be overcome, and people began to say, 'Yes, this can work.'"

Worth the Time and Investment

"It's important that the training is done up front, and not after you've started to become a team," said Travis.

"More is better," said Leader-Facilitator Norma Conklin. "As frightening as empowerment is to traditional managers, it's just as frightening to employees who've worked under the old system. They need as much training as they can get."

"Training takes time," said Jones. "You can't just throw it at everybody, because they can't absorb it all at once. As they move along the path, you deliver more training."

"Reenforcing training is very important," said York. "It's all well and good to participate in training, but if people don't see it applied, they'll feel it's a waste of their time."

Said Leader-Facilitator Juanita Harris, "It's worthwhile to spend the money for training, although up front it may look as if it isn't worth it. If we hadn't had training, we would still be trying to get started."

"The attitude in our division," said Travis, "is that we're committed to empowerment, and we're going to put our money where our mouth is. Training is expensive, but it's a necessary expense."

Empowered Results

Continued Travis, "Our self-esteem has taken a giant boost because we're really doing this."

Said Baumgardner, "We've just done another communications

survey. The new data shows we've made real strides. People feel better about their jobs and are excited and more involved. And even though we have budget constraints and our staff level has dropped, our productivity is up."

Said Hoffman, "Our non-exempt staff see new opportunities. They've been working at the same jobs for years and, all of a sudden, they're taking more of a leadership role because that's available. They've improved in morale. And they've come up with more ideas."

Added Baumgardner, "We're getting better responses on issues that were difficult in the past. Things like staff decisions and performance reviews, which teams are involved in now. One team wrote their own reviews."

Added Hoffman, "Teams are realizing that they can question policies. For example, one group found there wasn't a policy requiring five, eight-hour days a week, Monday through Friday. So they consulted with timekeeping and instituted alternate work schedules."

Said Division Director Griffith, "We've had statistical measures in place for ten years. We've watched these and found that we haven't lost ground, even though our work increased. Our customer satisfaction has historically been 98%. And since we started empowerment, it's 98 to 100%."

"Empowerment is a great business decision," added Dew. "If you're going to maximize your profits, you've got to maximize the amount of work people do, and that means maximizing their participation in the decision-making process. This allows you to redistribute your middle-management resources."

Top Priority: Training

"A lot of the nitty-gritty of team building is helping people work together and build trust," said TQM Specialist Audrey Byrd. "That doesn't just happen. You can intellectually make the leap and say, 'That's the way I'd like to work.' But working every day to help people resolve their conflicts takes a lot of effort. That's where the rubber meets the road.

"And that's why we made the commitment to make training our staff in empowered ways a top priority."

Date of Case Study: February, 1993

1997 Epilogue: "We've experienced one reorganization after another since 1993," said Donna Griffith, "including the merger in March, 1995 which resulted in Lockheed-Martin Corporation. And now there's a study under way that may result in our becoming part of a new, privately-held services company. We have reengineered, redesigned, consolidated, split, transferred, downsized, and we've looked at privatization. There isn't an organization that hasn't been affected, including ours which is now called Information Management Services.

"Through all of this, empowerment has not only survived, it's become necessary for survival. There are far fewer managers and there's a greater span of control, so managers have found they must empower people to get the work done and meet customer demands. The parts of the organization where we'd made the greatest progress in terms of empowerment, have been better equipped to deal with the onslaught of changes. We feel fortunate that we made the investment in empowerment when we did.

"In 1993, we started something called the Empowerment Champions Group—an informal network of those who were trying to do the same thing. We saw that there were other islands doing it and have made some significant progress in encouraging the spread of empowerment throughout our Oak Ridge facilities.

"Self-managed teams continued expanding for awhile, but we're more focused now on individual empowerment. With the spans of control being what they are, individuals are being asked to be more entrepreneurial and some groups are operating more independently but don't call themselves self-managed teams.

"Morale is understandably lower than four years ago, because of the layoffs we've had, but customer satisfaction is as high or higher

—despite the changes and increased pressure on people. We're now focusing our energies on the exciting opportunity to privatize our business, and we know that our empowerment experiences will serve us well in that new venture."

11

Communicating Empowerment at Federal Express

PROFILE

Organization: Federal Express, world's largest air express transportation company.
History: Began operations April 17, 1973, with an eight-plane fleet delivering eight packages.
Service: Delivers more than 1.6 million items daily to 180 countries.
Fleet: More than 455 aircraft; 30,000 computer- and-radio-equipped vehicles.
Employees: 94,000.
Location: Transportation hub/corporate headquarters in Memphis, Tennessee
Sales: More than $7.5 billion, with about 43% of air express market.
Malcolm Baldrige National Quality Award: 1990 recipient; was first service organization winner.

* * * * *

Twenty years ago, Federal Express Chairman and CEO Frederick W. Smith created a revolutionary new service industry: time-definite overnight package delivery. What he and most people probably didn't realize then, however, was that the company was also one of the pioneers of a new revolutionary management style: employee empowerment.

From day one, Federal Express has had to give its front-line employees wide decision-making power to keep its guarantee to customers: *Your package is delivered on time, or you don't pay.*

Then, as now, Federal Express found that communication was absolutely imperative. And today, it has invested billions of dollars in high-tech communications systems and communications techniques.

Jean Ward-Jones, Manager of quality education and administration, and Roy Golightly, director of employee communications, talked about how the company empowers through communication.

Laying the Foundation

"People-Service-Profit has been the corporate philosophy from the beginning," said Golightly. "And this has made us an industry leader. We make a large investment in our people because if we keep our employees informed, motivated and well-trained, they'll provide the service that customers expect.

"This in turn provides the profits for the corporation, which allow us to devote more to people. So you have a continuous cycle. People-Service-Profit are all interwoven."

Added Ward-Jones, "There is no success without customer satisfaction, and no customer satisfaction without employee satisfaction. So, from the beginning, Federal Express has put programs in place that drive employee satisfaction. Every time a decision is made, the first question asked is, 'How does this affect our employees?'

"You can pay people to do a job and they do it many ways," continued Ward-Jones. "They may do only what they need to, to keep their job. Or they may put forth more effort because they're competing with a few other people. Or they may put their entire heart, body and soul into the job and perform to the absolute best of their ability. Every time an employee interacts with a customer, the customer can tell which way the employee is doing the job.

"It's one thing to have empowerment on a manufacturing line, where you have the power to stop the line if something comes by that you don't like. It's something else again to have the majority of Federal Express' 94,000 people in direct contact with customers every day. If employees don't feel like giving them everything they should to satisfy the customer, the customer will know it."

What Empowerment Means

Said Golightly, "Empowerment for us means our employees know they have the power to make the decision to do whatever it takes to meet or exceed the customer's requirements.

"Their autonomy is what couriers and front-line employees like most about their jobs—being on their own and being able to make decisions without many pressures, policies and procedures. They consider their work like their own business.

"For example, a customer may tell a courier that instead of the usual three packages, he has 400 because of a special promotion. The courier has deadlines to meet. There are many ways he can handle this situation, but he has to make the decision.

"He can call for additional resources, if necessary. But if the dispatcher says no other resources are available, the courier has to figure out other options. He can't phone a supervisor and say, 'Hey, what do I do now?'"

Explained Ward-Jones, "To support this autonomy, the company has eliminated the title 'supervisor.' Our people don't get supervised. Couriers are on their own and have to accept this challenge without feeling that whatever happens, a supervisor will take care of it.

"Our money-back guarantee also supports autonomy. If we don't deliver the package within 60 seconds of when we said we would, or if we can't tell you where the package is within 30 minutes of your call—you get your money back. So if our couriers and customer service agents don't have the power to do whatever it takes to make that happen, we don't make money. And that affects everyone's pocket.

"When we first decided to use the 'absolutely, positively overnight' line in our advertising, our ad firm said, 'If you can't deliver on this promise, this campaign will ruin you.' Our executive management kept the language in the ad because they knew our people would make it happen.

"For example, one station had already locked up for the night and management had gone home," continued Ward-Jones. "All of a sudden, a customer came with his payroll in hand. He had had computer problems and couldn't finish the payroll on time.

"No managers were at the station to give instructions. So, the agent decided to send the checks. But they were were from a major company and were going many places. And he had a schedule to keep. Our pilot's job description doesn't include processing packages. Nonetheless, even the plane crew pitched in and helped get them ready and loaded on the plane.

"Not only did the employees accommodate the customer's needs, they also got the plane out on time. This was clearly above and beyond duty."

Said Golightly, "Empowerment has been ingrained in our culture from day one. There were heroes as much in the early days as there are now. Some pilots so believed in this dream that they sold their watches to buy fuel to keep the dream alive.

"And because overnight express was such a new service, empowerment was carte blanche for the people selling the service. They said, 'We have to do everything we can to get people to believe in us.' They did whatever it took. Today, one of our challenges is to keep that level of empowerment going."

Added Ward-Jones, "We have many employees who've never worked anyplace else. So, if you asked them what it means to be empowered, they may not know. This is the only atmosphere they've ever lived in.

"We've only recently begun using the term 'empowerment,' so it may be meaningless to them. They won't know what it means until, or unless, they get into a more traditional environment where they're expected to wait until they're told what to do, as opposed to figuring that out on their own."

Goals, Bonuses and Recognition

"One way we communicate empowerment is through our goals

and bonuses," said Golightly. "We simplified our bonus structure years ago by tying goals to our People-Service-Profit philosophy. If the corporation doesn't meet them, there are no management bonuses. In fact, we went without bonuses the year we won the Baldrige award."

The three goals are: 1) People—the continuous improvement of the management leadership index score, which is tracked through an annual Survey Feedback Action program; 2) Service—100 percent customer satisfaction, measured by Service Quality Indicators, known as the SQI index; and 3) Profit.

"There are also recognition and bonus opportunities for our front-line people," said Ward-Jones. "These include the Bravo Zulu, Golden Falcon and Circle of Excellence awards and Pay-for-Performance.

"The purpose of the Bravo Zulu is to catch people doing things right and give them immediate feedback. Our CEO was a marine pilot in the Vietnam War, and when a pilot lands successfully on an aircraft carrier, the person bringing him in gives him a Bravo Zulu ('well done') flag signal. Fred Smith brought that concept to Federal Express.

"We have stickers with the Bravo Zulu symbol," she continued. "For example, I might put one on a note to an employee that signifies a really good effort. We also have Bravo Zulu pins and plaques.

"Any manager also has authority to give a Bravo Zulu award of $100. Managers use the award for something directly benefitting the employee, such as a blank check to take their spouse to dinner, or tickets to a concert." Annually, the company gives more than 20,000 Bravo Zulus, totaling $1.8 million.

The Golden Falcon, the company's most prestigious award, is named for Federal Express' first airplanes. A committee meets quarterly or monthly to select people who truly represent heroes at Federal Express. Honorees receive company stock.

The Circle of Excellence applauds teamwork and is a monthly award given to top-performing stations.

Pay-for-performance is a merit raise based on individual performance, which managers evaluate periodically.

Daily Operations Meetings and Television Link-up

Communications are so vital at Federal Express that the company has an Employee Communications department of 60 people and spends about $50 per employee annually on print and audiovisual programs.

"We see our front-line managers as the cornerstone of communications," explained Golightly. "It's very important that they conduct routine meetings with employees to let them know what happened the previous day and what the focus should be that day."

Explained Ward-Jones, "A corporate Operations Meeting takes place daily at 8:30 a.m. We have a worldwide conference call in which representatives from our 12 divisions discuss major operational problems that occurred during the last 24 hours."

Operations information is also communicated through a five-minute show aired on the company's satellite-linked television network, FXTV.

Explained Golightly, "The program is largely an operational system review of how many packages we handled the day before, what the service level was, what sort of hub, aircraft, or other delays happened. The show is a planning tool, in that it forewarns people of problems they may face that day. We start broadcasting at 5:30 in the morning, Memphis time, and automatically turn on every site—more than 1200—so that the show is recorded and goes into continuous playback mode. It's ready to be viewed the minute people start work.

"We have also broadcast officers and directors meetings, which are strategic updates, twice a year. And we periodically broadcast a show called One-on-One, which is usually an interview with our CEO, Fred Smith."

Communicating Through Quality Boards

Empowerment also is communicated through the Executive

Quality Board (EQB) and the Quality Advisory Board (QAB). The EQB is chaired by the Vice President of Internal Audit and Quality, and is made up of senior management from each division. It functions as a steering board.

The QAB meets bi-weekly and consists of the division quality administrators and employee-involvement facilitators.

"We have 100 quality professionals around the world," explained Ward-Jones. "Their full-time responsibility is to train, coach, and facilitate employees in using quality processes, tools, and techniques.

"The boards and the quality professionals determine quality issues, the direction quality should take, and what progress we're making on our quality journey."

Quality Action Teams

Quality Action Teams (QATs) are 4-10-member problem-solving teams, often comprised of both management and hourly employees from different work groups or divisions. QATs are also formed across divisions to improve internal customer satisfaction. Working on an ad hoc or ongoing basis, QATs identify problems, pinpoint root causes, develop and implement action plans, and track down the effectiveness of solutions. At any one time, more than 1000 QATs are working on problem-solving. These are autonomous, but are often guided by quality administrators and facilitators.

Quarterly, each division chooses its best QAT quality success story. Considered the "best of the best," the QATs present their stories to CEO Smith and senior management. Entries are also published in the monthly Manager's Pak magazine.

Root Cause Teams have also been formed for each of the company's 12 SQI's, to study problems related to such indicators as abandoned phone calls, reopened complaints and damaged or lost packages. Knowledge of these indicators is another way of communicating to employees the importance of quality.

Communicating Empowerment Through Training

"There is no way you could empower employees without training," said Ward-Jones. "We spend close to 3% of our revenues on training. You can't empower employees until they know how to do the job and have all the resources they need.

"Most new customer-contact employees don't even see a customer until they've had from three to six weeks of training, depending upon their jobs.

"We also have recurrent training for all others to make sure they maintain the skills they need. Managers take a test on our Manager's Guide annually so they don't forget what it means to be a manager and leader. Every manager also is required to take a minimum of 40 hours of training a year.

"We try to make sure managers, officers, and directors are really wired into what total quality is all about," continued Ward-Jones. "They've all gone through three days of training in quality basics and QAT techniques. We've also developed video courses on the customer-supplier alignment process and on benchmarking. And we've created a textbook.

"We also developed a course called 'Blueprint for Systematic Quality' that turns the Baldrige categories into a diagnostic tool for management in each operational area. This is designed to determine the gaps between where we are and where we want to be."

Survey Feedback

One of the company's most important empowerment communications is the annual Survey Feedback Action (SFA) program. Part of the quality process for the past 12 years, the survey gives employees a chance to tell anonymously how they feel about the company, their managers, and about the service, pay, and benefits.

The results are compiled and passed on to managers, who must then meet with work groups to form a written action plan for resolving any problems. All the work group results also are tallied into an overall corporate leadership score. This is used to diagnose corporate-wide leadership problems and becomes part of management's overall objectives. SFA is a problem-solving device that's used horizontally and vertically throughout the organization.

Guaranteed Fair Treatment

Every Tuesday, CEO Smith and four other top executives meet to review and rule on employee complaints through the company's Guaranteed Fair Treatment Procedure (GFTP). At a Board of Review, the employee's peers, as well as management, are final arbiters of justice.

In addition to GFTP, "Open Door" is a policy-and-procedure feedback process that provides a pathway to management for employee complaints/questions regarding global corporate policies. These concern such things as benefits, hiring, seniority, and the like.

Super Tracker

"We're very technologically oriented," explained Golightly, "not for technology's sake, but because we're continually listening and monitoring our customer's needs. Customers have told us they want as much information as we can give them. So, we invested billions of dollars in technology for things like our Cosmos II-B Super Tracker, which our couriers helped design, and our digitally-assisted dispatch systems.

"These are demonstrations of empowerment because they tell employees we'll give them the tools to satisfy the customer."

Other Communications

Continued Golightly, "Knowledge and information are power. Our job is to give as much information as possible, about everything to everybody. Our philosophy is to be the first to tell our employees about our company. The worst possible thing is to read in the newspaper something about your company that affects your life, and the company has done nothing to tell you about it. We absolutely refuse to let that happen. We go to great lengths to maintain open communication.

"To do this, we produce about 22 different newsletters, each geared to specific segments of the employee base, such as newsletters for just pilots or couriers. We also have corporate publications, including our monthly magazine, *Worldwide Update,* and our publication *This Week at Federal Express.*"

Lessons Learned

"You can't do enough communicating," said Golightly. "Also, you can communicate empowerment as a philosophy, but you have to tie it into a broader concept. You have to explain why it's important. We're in business to maintain and attract customers every day.

"We have to explain everything we do in this context. For example, why do we ask an employee to code a package on our Super Tracker? What is the big picture of that action? When you explain, people buy into what you're telling them better."

Said Ward-Jones, "There used to be a saying that you could buy quality, or time, or low cost. But you could never get all three in the same purchase. Well, globalization is changing that. Today, if you don't meet the quality gate you're not going to be in the marketplace. Time and cost then become the competitive issues and they are determined by the degree of quality.

"With things changing as dramatically as they do at Federal Express, if we had to wait for employees to get instructions, nothing would ever happen. That's why employees must be empowered."

Date of Case Study: March, 1993

1997 Epilogue: "We're continuing to use the communication vehicles that were mentioned in the case study," said Ed Robertson, Manager of Employee Communication at Federal Express. "During the intervening period, we've also focused a lot on change and on leadership within the company, recognizing that we have to embrace change and become more effective leaders; otherwise we'll atrophy and not be able to meet the demands of the market place.

"Recently, we've begun to put much more emphasis on the communication process inside each of our approximately 7,000 work groups—making communication more of a management process—because business pressures are such that communication in the future must work at extremely efficient and effective levels. It's an initiative called Managerial Communication Competence (MCC) that's being rolled out first in areas where vice presidents feel improvement is needed in the communication between our employees and first-level managers—which is often picked up by our early warning system, Survey-Feedback-Action. MCC will eventually reach the entire company.

"MCC has five components. The first is awareness, which addresses something we call the Open and Supportive Communication Model. The model sets out the new expectations which go well beyond just saying that communication is very important, to spelling out what should be done behaviorally to meet that responsibility. The model contains five information-sharing practices and 11 interpersonal communication skills, such as checking accuracy, clarifying meaning, soliciting and giving feedback and managing conflict. The model is central, because the assessment and training are based on it.

"The other four components are: assessment, which includes both an employee communication survey and a report for the manager; training, which is a one-day experiential workshop; removing impediments, which, for example, includes encouragement for managers to meet regularly in work group meetings with their employees; and evaluation, which calls for vice presidents to use the MCC model and particular communication elements as measures during managerial performance reviews.

"Efficient and effective communication relates directly to empowerment, because with it employees will be flexible and free to make decisions that will serve our customers well and will keep us a viable and successful company."

12

Empowerment at Zytec: Letting Go and Taking Charge

PROFILE

Organization: Zytec Corp., an employee-owned company (formerly a division of Control Data Corporation).
History: In business more than 25 years. Began operating independently in 1984 after a leveraged buyout.
Products: Power supplies for original equipment manufacturers of computers, electronic office, medical and test equipment. Also repairs cathode-ray tube monitors and power supplies.
Employees: 748
Location: Headquartered in Eden Prairie, a suburb of Minneapolis. Manufacturing facility at Redwood Falls, Minnesota, 96 miles southwest.
Sales: About $73 million.
Awards: Since 1987, received nine awards for supplier excellence, including one of only two IBM Market-Driven Quality Awards, Gold Level. Also won 1991 Malcolm Baldrige National Quality Award, 1991 Minnesota Quality Award and 1992 *Industry Week's* Best Plants Award.

* * * * *

Zytec Corp. would be the first to admit it hasn't yet reached nirvana when it comes to employee empowerment. But it gives employees far greater freedom in decision-making than most businesses do today, and involves employees more in total company operations.

If the truth be known, however, empowerment at Zytec was not so much a matter of choice as it was a matter of circumstances. On the brink of going out of business in 1985, this leading power supply company owes its survival today to a paradigm shift in which managers learned to "let go" and give employees the power to "take charge."

John M. Steel, vice president of marketing and sales, explained the evolution. "Our empowerment crusade was aided by two things. First, we experienced an information dissemination revolution. In the past, only managers could go to the computer center for information, and they would parcel out information in bits and pieces. No one had the big picture, except them.

"Today, with distributed data processing, all Zytec employees have access to computers and terminals and can call up virtually everything on the database. They don't have to ask anyone's permission.

"Zytec is an employee-owned company, with about 400 employees owning stock. Every employee has an option to buy 1,000 shares after a year with the company. Some senior employees can buy more. Zytec made a commitment to employees that nothing is private.

"The second thing that hit us was that in 1985 we almost lost the company. When Zytec was founded, we were 100 percent dedicated to Control Data Corp. After the leveraged buyout, the race was on to get more business from other companies before Control Data left us. But their business started declining faster than we were getting outside business. In 1984 our revenue was $66 million. In 1985, it dropped to $42 million.

"That was an extremely painful experience. We would like to say our empowerment crusade has been one of beauty and nirvana, but we've been through hell. We had 20 percent pay cuts for senior staff, 10 percent pay cuts for others, workforce reductions and layoffs. We were forced by the reality of the marketplace to cut back if we were to compete and survive.

"In 1984, we had about 500 employees and 57 managers. Today we have more than 700 employees and just 33 managers. When you reduce the number of managers, somebody still has to make the decisions. Because of information dissemination, we could turn a lot of the decision-making process over to employees."

Giving Employees the Tools

"Empowerment requires both managers who are willing to let go, and employees who have the knowledge, tools and skills to assume responsibilities," continued Steel. "You don't decide on Friday that you're going to empower people, and on Monday say, 'Now hear this. You're all empowered.' You've got to give them the tools, knowledge and training. And you have to tolerate mistakes; so you're putting yourself at risk.

"To prepare our employees, we've done some very formal and some informal training. We conduct a minimum of 133 hours of mandatory training for all employees during their first three years of employment. We also reward production employees for Multi-Functional Employee training, increasing their pay for demonstrated proficiency in new tasks."

Signs of Empowerment/Trust

"We went for W. Edwards Deming's 14 Points for Management hook, line and sinker," continued Steel. "And they work. He invites you to believe in the worth and dignity of the individual. To trust. It made incredible sense to us.

"The employees looked for signs of empowerment and saw some interesting signs early. One concerned our tool crib. Deming says, 'Buy the best tools money can buy and break down barriers.' We got it half right. We bought the best tools, but we put them in a tool crib with a tool crib attendant.

"Even long-time employees couldn't get tools. Take this hypothetical case, for example. An employee is a farm wife with a

$125,000 combine and who has raised six children. Yet when she breaks the end off her Phillips screwdriver, she has to fill out a four-part form and go through six layers of management fat. And finally, when she goes to the tool crib attendant, he says, 'What are you doing here? I gave you your tools ten years ago.'

"Why was he doing that? Because management had told him that last year he used $50,000 in tools and he would be a hero if we only used $40,000. So he was following the system and making sure the tools were not made available to employees.

"Today there is no tool crib, or attendant, or forms, or layers of management approval. The best tools money can buy are lying in open cabinets. And if an employee needs a screwdriver, he or she can get it without asking permission. When that tool crib fence came down, what did that say to the employees about trust?

"Sure, some of our tools have probably been stolen. But instead of spending the time and money trying to protect Zytec from the one- or two-percent abuse, we changed the system. I guarantee you that the tools we lose don't equal the attendant's salary. And if we find a thief, there's no discussion or theft therapy. We terminate the employee.

"Another sign employees saw was the elimination of management perks, like designated parking spaces. Today if you get to work first, you park near the door. If you're last, you walk—no matter who you are.

"In the past, we had time cards and quotas and labor variance reporting. We've thrown all that out. Now, employees only use time cards when they work more or less than 40 hours.

"No individual bonuses are paid out at the end of the year. And we eliminated individual performance incentives for our sales force.

"We also have flexible hours. And we have employee-managed time off. Employees accrue vacation and sick hours each month for time off and determine how they'll use them. It's an honor system.

"Another honor system is our Powerbusters employee club. The club stocks the mini-cafeteria with coffee, soft drinks, and snacks and marks the prices. There's a place for employees to leave their money. Sometimes the count comes up short, and sometimes it's over."

Management by Planning

Zytec employees are also empowered through Management By Planning (MBP), which is an interactive process initiated in 1988 to develop a five-year strategic plan and short-term objectives. MBP starts with six cross-functional teams that represent Zytec's 33 departments. These teams set five-year plans for Marketing and Sales, Manufacturing, Materials, Personnel, Engineering and Administration.

At an annual two-day meeting, about 150 employees, representing all types of personnel, shifts and departments, join with customers and suppliers to review the plans. Then, with this input, Zytec CEO Ronald D. Schmidt and senior executives finalize the plan and determine four objectives for the next year.

"The four objectives are cascaded into the organization," explained Steel. "Each department sets four objectives to support those of the company and forms four teams—one for each objective. So we have about 136 teams, with about 85% of our employees participating.

"Once a month, department representatives meet in Redwood Falls with senior management for a 9-hour operations review. Some teams are making breakthrough progress and their results are absolutely dramatic. Others are stuck. They're using fishbone diagrams when they should be using Paretos. Or, they haven't defined the process. We celebrate the success of teams that are doing well and work with those who need help.

"The employees measure us [managers] by our performance, how we spend our time, our calendar. We spend anywhere from 25 to 50% on quality improvement."

What Empowerment Means to Zytec Employees

Zytec employees are given broad authority to achieve team and personal goals. For example, any employee has the power to spend $1,000 to solve a customer complaint without prior approval; hourly workers can make changes with the agreement of only one other person; and sales people can travel whenever they feel it is necessary for customer service.

Explained Bill Newfield, sales representative, "Employees have the ability to solve a problem, no questions asked. They know their jobs the best, so they're the persons most likely to know how to solve problems.

"For example, before voice mail was available, one of my West Coast customers complained that he couldn't reach me after hours. So I bought three answering machines for myself and two other sales representatives who were having the same problem. I sent the bill to John Steel."

"Empowerment is also knowing that no matter what you do to solve the problem, management and Zytec are behind you, even if your decision is wrong," said Becky Miller, Quotation Analyst for Marketing and Sales. "You don't have to be afraid you're going to lose your job."

"If we see something that needs to be done, we can do it," said Linda Peterson, Documentation Control. "Such a simple thing like planting flowers in the spring. We'll buy the flowers and give John the receipt. We carry this through in every aspect of our jobs."

Recalled Miller, "A few years ago, one of my two children was ill and had to be hospitalized often. Zytec arranged to put a FAX machine, computer and private phone line in my home, so I could still work and be with my sick child. My child is no longer sick, but the equipment is still there and I work at home when necessary."

Said Nita Nelson, Production, "There are a lot of cases where people have taken their computers home to do work they couldn't get finished at Zytec. I've taken my winding machine home and all my supplies to finish work for the repair shop."

"You can even take things home for personal use," said Jerry Masog, Shipping and Receiving, "I took home an extension ladder to do some painting."

"Another example of empowerment concerns a trade show in Atlanta," recalled Miller. "I got a call on Sunday from the Zytec rep telling me some pamphlets and brochures hadn't been shipped. I couldn't get them to Atlanta by Monday morning on the usual shipping flights, so I purchased a one-way ticket on Northwest and put the box of materials on a passenger seat. I didn't hesitate and think I needed approval. I just bought the ticket and sent the bill to John."

"We've also broken down barriers," said Molly Schoephoerster, buyer/planner in Purchasing. "If I have a question to direct to an external customer, I can bypass the salesman and go to the customer directly. There's a good enough relationship that I won't have a problem getting my question answered."

Said Newfield, "A lot of times people get caught up in blaming somebody when something goes wrong. Instead, we focus on the process. If something goes wrong, you don't blame the person. You fix the process. It's not a question of someone not trying hard enough, or not doing something right. It's that the process doesn't allow you to handle the situation correctly. This mentality has done a lot for empowerment here. People are willing to take chances to do whatever is needed to get their jobs done."

Recalled Marty Glenn, senior development technician, "I had been with the company only two years, yet they allowed me and my partner, Larry Funari, to spend $180,000 to build an automated equipment tester. We had been doing our prototype testing on the bench, manually. Some tests required 20,000 measurements.

"We decided to automate. But when we got bids from five vendors, either the prices were way too high, or they couldn't meet our every need. I had had some experience with automated testing. And Larry and I felt we could put something together ourselves, so we took it to management in MBP. Our purpose was to reduce cycle time.

"One vendor had quoted $429,000. Another quote was $320,000. We spent $180,000. It was a big commitment by management, but the first time we plugged the tester in, it worked. Chances of that happening are slim. Now we test in a matter of minutes, instead of days. We've reduced cycle time from 12 to 4 weeks."

Executives Work the Line

"Zytec has a program called the Implemented Improvement System that encourages employees to contribute ideas," said Schoephoerster. "When your idea is implemented, you submit it and receive a dollar. At the end of the month, a review board evaluates the ideas and awards $100 for first place, $75 for second and $50 for third. The names of all employees whose ideas were implemented are then placed in a drawing to receive a day off with pay. The winner chooses an executive to work his or her position. Even Ron Schmidt, our CEO, has worked on the line."

"Often the employee doesn't take the day off," added Steel. "He or she doesn't want us to screw up the job. So they hang around and watch. They're not going to trust their customers to us managers."

Self-managed Teams

"Our teams in Zytec run the spectrum," said Steel. "Some production teams have one manager leading 50 employees. We also have about six or seven self-managed teams and are looking for more.

"For example, when the manager of our account management team in Redwood Falls was promoted and transferred, we chose not to replace him. We turned all authority for the team over to the employees. They report to me once a month, so I can learn how they're doing and can help if processes need improving.

"But they decide all the rest—their travel, travel expenses, time cards, priorities. If time cards are required, they sign them for each other. They put together their own departmental budget."

New Product Development Teams

"We have about 30 employees on New Product Development

Teams working on about 15-18 new product development programs," continued Steel. "For example, we have two engineering development teams working with a customer to design power supplies for the next generation of their equipment.

"The teams consist of representatives from our customers, Engineering, Materials and Manufacturing and the Sales and Account representatives. Usually there is one manager and the rest are employees. They meet weekly by teleconferencing."

Explained John Beecroft, project manager, "We meet just to make sure everyone knows what's going on between engineering in Eden Prarie, manufacturing in Redwood Falls and at our customer sites. We keep up to date and also keep reconfirming our schedule commitments. The meetings are brief—some just a few minutes and most not more than a half hour. The details and problems are resolved outside of the meetings.

"Everyone can chip in with their particular concern. For example, if a customer says they have a problem with a product fitting into their system, a mechanical engineer may say, 'I can change that, but it will have a two-week impact.' The account manager is worried because of the schedule. So at that moment, everyone knows exactly what problems arise because of the change, and we'll hammer out a solution."

Employee Visits to Customers

"We're very fortunate at Zytec in that we have identifiable customers and products," said Steel. "They're not nameless and faceless. For example, our Team Abbott employees know they're making products for Abbott in Texas. A number of Zytec employees have visited there. And when Abbott comes here, they meet with Team Abbott employees—whether it's lunch with pizza, or hot dogs and hamburgers in the park. When we receive awards, we make sure the sun shines on the employees who made it happen.

"This year, more than 260 Zytec production workers paid visits to customer sites. When two or three production employees spend a day at Abbott with their peers, Abbott is no longer a distant place in Dallas. It has names and faces. The Abbott and Zytec employees laugh together at lunch and talk about their kids and mortgages. So now Zytec employees have friends at Abbott that they don't want to disappoint in respect to quality and on-time delivery. They're not working for Zytec, they're working for Abbott Labs.

"In addition, we sent a production team to IBM for a couple of days to build computers, and they sent a production team here to build power supplies."

The Proof Is in the Results

Since 1985, Zytec's product quality has risen to the Four-Sigma range, putting it on track for Six Sigma in 1995. Mean-time-between failure exceeded 1.5 million hours for new products during 1991. The industry average is 750,000.

There was a five-year reduction of 72% in warranty costs. On-time delivery performance improved 22% in warranty costs. On-time delivery performance improved 22% since 1990, to 98%. Scrap/rework has been reduced 66% in the past five years to 0.23% of sales. And during the 1991 recession, revenue growth was 28%.

They'll Delight You

"Empowerment is scary. You get surprised," concluded Steel. "From the negative side, when you turn power over to employees, they sometimes make mistakes you could have avoided if you had been micro-managing the process. Sometimes they waste money going down blind alleys that, with your experience and wisdom, you could have helped them avoid. And sometimes they embarrass the company—but that's such a small percentage of the time.

"For the most part, if you trust them, they'll delight you."

Date of Case Study: November, 1992

1997 Epilogue: "We've about doubled in size and profits are up since the case study was written," reports John Steel. "And as a result of the company going public in November 1993, the stock splitting and the stock price climbing, our employees have had the opportunity to make a lot of money on their exercised stock options—that's about $20,000 to $100,000 each.

"We're still carrying forward the empowerment crusade. Management by Planning is going strong, with the emphasis on quality, cycle time, customer service and costs. We have many more self-managed teams throughout the company, including our main manufacturing facility in Redwood Falls, Minnesota and our two new facilities in Austria and Broomfield, Colorado, each of which has a couple of hundred employees. And we've added more tools, like e-mail, a Web site, voice mail and cellular phones to facilitate information exchange and to allow knock-your-socks-off service to come alive.

"Recently, we reaffirmed Zytec's original 1984 value statement, adding some key words which further ingrain the concept of empowerment: teamwork, mutual trust and involvement.

"We still want our quality to be at world class levels and to be the best power sources company in the world—not the biggest, the best. Empowerment is essential to making that happen."

13

The Plant Manager as Change Agent at Monsanto Chemical

PROFILE

Organization: Pensacola Plant Site, one of eight chemical plants of Monsanto Chemical Group, a division of the Monsanto Corporation.
Products: Nylon fiber for carpets and tires, and chemicals used in producing nylon, such as nitric acid, adipic acid and maleic anhydride. World's largest manufacturing unit for production of nitric acid and maleic anhydride.
Customers: Carpet, tire and nylon producers.
Employees: 1,700 Monsanto and 700 to 900 contract workers; non-union.
Location: Since 1953, located on a 2,500-acre site near Pensacola, Florida, including a golf course, shooting range, electricity generating plant, and 1,000 acres dedicated to a wildlife preserve.

* * * * *

It's a given that making a profit is the main reason for being in business. So it's not surprising that in 1985, after Monsanto's Pensacola chemical plant kept coming up short on the bottom line, the parent company in St. Louis issued an ultimatum: we must return to normal profitability.

Like many other companies that have had a similar wake-up call, Pensacola immediately began to scrutinize the way they were operating. It was clear they had to change. But the question was how? And if change was possible, could they transform themselves quickly enough to turn the profitability around?

A decade later, the Pensacola plant has proved that positive change was indeed possible. Today they're a thriving plant that, among other achievements, has seen a 65% improvement in what used to be called "hourly" employee productivity, a 30% improvement in salaried productivity, and annual gainsharing of multi-millions of dollars in the past two years.

Monsanto Pensacola's turnaround was a result of radical restructuring of the organization and putting new work processes in place since 1985. The leadership style of plant manager Lee Hebert has been one of the keys to its success. Hebert shared how the change was achieved and talked about its impact on the business.

Five Significant Changes Made the Difference

"Over the past decade, five significant changes took place in our plant," recalled Hebert. "They were a commitment to teams in 1985; assessment of the organization in 1989; establishment of product teams versus hierarchy in 1991; restructuring rewards and recognition in 1993; and a nonexempt redesign effort in 1994.

"The pivotal point came in 1985 when the company offered a retirement incentive. Out of 113 first-line supervisors, 87 accepted the incentive. Because our goal was to build the plant of the 90's, which would be focused on teams, we didn't replace the retiring supervisors.

"Instead, we brought in consultants to help us redesign our work and a group of employees went offsite to develop the 'how.' Based on their recommendation, we began a Total Quality initiative. Our focus was productivity and improvement teams, with our goal self-directed teams. We also instituted Computer-Integrated Manufacturing and committed the entire plant to Provox Computer Control.

"To bring about these changes, we made a commitment to our management that we would increase productivity 50 percent."

From Hierarchy to Product Teams

"By 1989, when I came to Pensacola as manager, the plant had achieved a 60% improvement in productivity," continued Hebert. "I was welcomed, however, with a flattening of the growth. Results had flattened and the challenge was to get the plant back on an upward track. We brought in a consultant to help us with an assessment. Their research showed that our middle management was not handing off everything they could to the lower levels of the organization.

"So we did a second assessment relative to team development to find out why. We learned that although we had a fairly good team organization at the bottom, there was a command-and-control hierarchy above that. It was a power issue. Most of our middle management had come up through the ranks. They had worked long and hard to get where they were and wouldn't give it up. We were not succeeding as a site team because we didn't see the value of pushing information and decisions down.

"In those days, I had a staff of eight people. We all agreed the organization needed changing, so I charged them to create the kind of organization they thought would help us get on track. In six months, they developed a plan. Basically, they had designed themselves out of their jobs. They recommended product teams, instead of the traditional hierarchy. With their plan, we went from the typical five-level organization to three levels: site manager, team leaders and the people who make the products.

"Today we have three business teams: Nylon Fibers Business Group, Chemicals Business Group, and Site Services Business Group. Each is a small business that runs as a team. As plant manager, I'm a kind of cheerleader for them.

"Because restructuring from a functional arrangement into these business groups was a huge transition, we needed someone to keep the focus on the transition process. So three of the original eight staff members became facilitators for the business groups. Of the remaining staff members, four retired and one became a plant manager at another Monsanto site. Our commitment was that the facilitators would be gone in three years. Only one of the three is gone so far. The reason is, they don't go until I get them good jobs within Monsanto."

Leveling the Playing Field

"Once teams were in place in the entire plant, we quickly found that we had to level the playing field so everyone could play," continued Hebert. "We had a pension plan for the hourly workforce and a different one for the salaried workforce. In 1993, we went to an all-salaried structure with benefits formulas the same for all.

"We also allowed people to choose their work shifts. We said that we didn't care what shift was worked, as long as they got their work done. In the past, accountants had said they couldn't manage more than one shift schedule. Today, we have five work schedules. And the plant is doing better than ever.

"In 1993, we also established gainsharing. Our plan is actually a hybrid between profit sharing and gainsharing. We first make our budget, then gainsharing gets funded. We have plant goals and business goals and there are take-aways if goals aren't reached. In our first year, we paid out multi-millions of dollars in gainsharing. For 1994, we paid out even more.

"Gainsharing has gotten more ideas for us than you could ever believe. Our people know they can make a difference, so they're involved. They want to make things happen. They're on the team.

"Diversity is also a big issue for us. In the past two years we've spent about $2 million on a diversity effort to try to level the playing field in that area. My message is that when you walk through the gate, I want you contributing at 125% and I'm going to find a way to tear down every barrier that won't allow you to do that.

"The next step in the process was to look at how we pay people. We're currently in a nonexempt redesign effort. Like most big companies, we've had pay raises every year. And, as a result, our compensation became noncompetitive in our industry. If we're going to be around for the next ten years, we've got to get this right.

"So we had a group of team leaders redesign our salary practices. In the past, an employee would be at the top rate of pay in our plant in 36 months. We've stretched that to ten years. Most of the increase will come in the first five. The folks already at the top will get smaller increases than competition until we are again competitive. This salary redesign doesn't seem like much; but it's a huge change for us.

"We're also changing how we hire people. Instead of training people in everything as we've done in the past, we're hiring the skills we want. If employees want to acquire a skill, they can take courses outside. Then, if they pass our test, they can work in their skill area. We are getting out of the basic training business. We will still do job-specific safety training."

Marketing Change to Corporate Headquarters

"We really faced a dilemma when we wanted to eliminate command-and-control and make other radical changes," explained Hebert. "Our corporate headquarters is made up of people who are good at hierarchy. So when we designed our new structure, we created a marketing plan to sell it to our corporate management. I went to St. Louis a number of times to sell our reorganization.

"One of the hardest groups to convince was the controllership group. They said, 'You mean we're not going to have one person responsible for the plant?' I said, 'No. You're going to have three people who are working through me. You're not going to have one controllership person.'

"In presenting our plan, the 'hook' was that we could improve salaried productivity by 30%. No one has ever addressed the traditional salaried team in this fashion before. At our site alone, a 30%

improvement would save millions of dollars per year. That was an offer our management couldn't refuse. Even though I don't believe they fully understood what we were doing, they said they couldn't afford not to try it.

"On July 1, 1993, we had another salary retirement incentive. The only way you could receive the incentive, however, was if your job wasn't replaced. That day, 93 people walked out of our plant and we didn't replace one. This alone resulted in a 35% improvement in traditional salaried productivity."

Getting Team Leaders to Hand Off Responsibility

"In the past, we had general superintendents, with each having as many as 500 people reporting to them," explained Hebert. "They were small-plant managers in a big plant. We did away with them and now have 55 team leaders—people who used to work for those superintendents and are now in charge. I gave each of them $75,000 in capital authority and said, 'Just sign your name and spend it. But make sure you spend it right.'

"How do you think the team leaders felt on the first day of the job? They said, 'You mean, when I make a decision, it's mine? I've got no buffer?' After three weeks into this change, they were on overload and were saying, 'I can't do all this.' I said, 'Terrific! You're right where you need to be. Remember what I told you about hand off? Hand off everything you can to the lowest level in the organization.'

"So the hand-off process began. Team leaders no longer had the luxury of holding onto everything. The buffers above them were gone. They needed to get things done, so they had to hand off to the lower levels.

"Coaching was the key to the new structure. Team leaders were given responsibilities they had never had before and they were forced to expand overnight. If you do that to people, they're going to struggle for awhile. When you make a change like this, you need a transition plan because you're not going to facilitate a change of this magnitude very easily.

"Changing is a learning process and you have to grow into it. It took a couple of years for team leaders to get comfortable with their new role. The coach [facilitator] was the key person in helping us through this transition.

"Going from superintendents to 55 teams created a greater environment for productivity. Team leaders have their own ideas and do what they want to, as long as it fits into our general business direction.

"When we implemented this change, folks in the plant couldn't believe management was going to give them what we did. At first, when they saw the eight best jobs going away, people wondered what career opportunities were left. My response was, 'We've just created 55 great jobs called Team Leader. Now instead of one out of eight, you've got one out of 55 chances for advancement.' Team leader is now the cherished job in our plant. So the new structure has created more opportunities for people who want growth. And what we got was credibility. People saw that we were serious about changing."

Trust Them: They'll Make the Same Decisions

"Originally, I had eight staff members. Then suddenly I was managing 55 team leaders," recalled Hebert. "How do you manage this large a staff? First, you've got to trust people. Hierarchy, with its command-and-control, doesn't require as much trust.

"Today if a team leader says he has to do something, I trust that he's made the right decision. If we can trust our team leaders and share every piece of information we have with them, I'm convinced they'll make the same decisions we would. They have the company's best interest at heart and want to do the right things. We also must be tolerant of failures, occasionally. We all grow through our mistakes.

"We also no longer conduct performance reviews for team leaders. Instead, we have an open appraisal session in which team leaders appraise themselves as part of their business group. Who better to do that than themselves? I can't know what 55 people are doing. But their peers know.

"With open appraisal, the team leaders of each business group meet and open-ended questions are asked to stimulate discussion. For example, we might ask, 'If it were your business, what would you have done differently last year?' Or, 'Pete, did the Organizational Development person make the necessary things happen for you so you could get that shift in place?' In this way, the business group evaluates what team leaders are doing."

Spending More than Half Time Communicating Pays Off

"Communications have been greatly enhanced," said Hebert. "Communicating down the organization was easy. Every Monday morning at 9:00, I would go to a site team leader meeting and tell them all I needed to. And they would share the information with the shop floor. But we struggled with getting team leaders to communicate upward.

"After I would talk about the business, no one would speak. With 55 people, the session was too big and just too threatening. So instead of the site meeting, we created a meeting for each business group and I attend all three. With these smaller sessions of 20 or fewer, we have two-way dialogue.

"Each business group also sends a representative to the other business groups so they can have linkage and know what each is doing.

"By streamlining communications, we now get done what we want, instead of having everything interpreted three or four times at different levels. Also, our team leaders are more involved with the business community. So we're building a customer focus at the same time.

"Another way of communicating is through personal meetings with everybody in the plant. I try to be in the plant 50-60% of the time with the people. This is very, very important in implementing change. I'll meet with an area team leader with 20 employees or fewer and spend whatever time it takes to convince them why we must do what we want to do.

"It takes an honest commitment to the open sharing of information. When I came to the plant in 1989, we had eight recordable injuries during my first ten days on the job. Now if you're safety conscious, as Monsanto is, that's disastrous. I made a decision to go into the plant in the next 30 days and speak to everyone about my commitment to safety. I failed. It took me 60 days because there were so many people.

"I told them we were going to be a zero injury plant. They thought I was a ludicrous nut. No plant this size would go without injuries. We had 49 recordable injuries in 1989. Last, year, we had seven. We're on the way to zero and now the conversation is, 'When will we get there?'

"I also told the people I would never lie to them. If I didn't know something, I would say I didn't know. And if they wanted the answer, I'd get it for them."

Conviction, More Than Courage, Brought Change

"The changes we introduced at Monsanto were the result of the breakthrough training I did some years ago," said Hebert. "The training changed my life because I suddenly began to focus on things I could do, not on things I could do nothing about.

"I had asked to manage a plant in Massachusetts so I could be near my elderly parents. Instead, Monsanto said they wanted me to run Pensacola, the biggest plant in the company. The plant was very large, with numerous people productivity opportunities, and my charge was to see what I could do about them. It was a challenge I couldn't refuse.

"When I came to Pensacola, I used the breakthrough concepts to make change happen because I could see frustration from the top to the bottom. The plant was Human Resources led, with many opportunities for improvement.

"First, we created a vision of where we wanted to go. Then we got people to buy into it, and we just took off and went with it. I don't think the changes were a matter of courage as much as they were of conviction. I really felt something could happen. It's been a great five years.

"Pensacola is a non-union plant. I believe, however that you can also implement radical change in a union plant, but it takes longer. The difference between a union and a nonunion plant is that the first has two agendas. For example, if I go into a non-union plant to convince the people of the value of what we want, it's done before I leave. However, if I do the same in a union plant, the people can't proceed until it's approved by the union. So they've got this second agenda.

"You have to work with unions just as you work with the entire organization. At West Virginia, we had one of the toughest unions in the world, the steel workers. We took them from a very militant environment to one in which we were committed to making them the best union.

"Bringing about change in a union plant takes longer because you've got both the organization and the union to satisfy. Once satisfied, the union can be a great driver for you. I don't think management has focused enough over the years on working through unions. I believe union leadership is changing today and wants to be a part of change. Our challenge as management is to take advantage of this desire on a win-win basis."

It's Difficult to Spread Success

"My biggest frustration," said Hebert, "is that I can't transfer this new approach even within our own company. Last year when we had our greatest year ever, I asked a high-level manager, 'Why don't you try this over at this plant, or that plant?' He said, 'I think we need one more year to be sure it works.' What's he going to say when our next year is even better?

"It's very difficult for upper leadership to be open to the possibility that the risk of change is worth taking when times are good. So if you're going to present organizational changes to them, you'd better have a hook that will get them on board—such as our 30% increase in salaried profitability. They need to see the value in taking the risk.

"Our Pensacola plant is one of total involvement and total commitment. What we have may not be the organization for the future, but it works. My message to others is that you should try to create the organization that will work for you. Do away with command-and-control. And, above all, trust people, make an honest commitment to open sharing of information, and let people show you what they are capable of accomplishing."

Date of Case Study: February 1995

1997 Epilogue: "During the last two years, we've continued to implement our organizational and compensation changes," said Lee Hebert. "The compensation structure should position us very well for the future. And our gainsharing continues to go well; we've had another excellent year in 1996 and should have another near-maximum payout.

"Organizationally, several things have been happening. First, we've outsourced some activities that aren't directly related to our core chemicals business. For example, instead of training all mechanics ourselves, we're hiring already-trained mechanics and promoting existing employees who take the initiative to get trained on the outside, which we will pay for.

"Second, we think it's time to redesign our organization again. Everything has its life span. This time, we're looking at how we can use values as the basis for our redesign and for where we want our business to be in the future. Our teams and the basics will definitely continue; we want to enhance what's in place.

"And, third, the chemical piece of Monsanto is going through a spin-off which we'll be part of. From an organizational design perspective, it appears a lot like what we've got here. So, the ideas are being transferred to the larger organization after all."

14

A Leader's Tool Kit for Transformation at Allstate

"I've often been asked how I learned to do this," said Jack Callahan, president of Allstate Business Insurance Group (ABIG), referring to the turnaround he led in his business unit since assuming leadership in 1989. "My answer is: By trial and error.

"Over the years, I've kept a file on things I've tried. Before I start a new job assignment, I go through the file to see what will work best in the coming situation. The file is my tool kit. What evolved from the trial and error were 18 Imperatives of Success, which I used at ABIG.

"And people also say to me, 'You've worked in Human Resources. That must have been where you learned this soft stuff.' Honestly, it came from the many experiences I've had. I've learned that the hard stuff—command-and-control—is the easy way. It's the soft stuff that's hard to do, but it's what really makes the difference."

Thanks to a variety of jobs in manufacturing and service, Callahan's tool kit gave him plenty of experiences to draw from. With a college degree in accounting and finance, his career began in engineering/purchasing at United Technologies' Pratt & Whitney Aircraft Division. Then in 1959, he joined Allstate at Hartford, Connecticut, where he served on and off for 17 years. His assignments were in sales, human resources, claims and many other areas.

In 1971, he was placed in charge of one of Allstate's 25 regions, with responsibility for thousands of employees. And he has managed large groups ever since. In 1982, he was named to Allstate's Board of

Directors. This month, after 35 years at Allstate, he is retiring—leaving with a special sense of achievement because of ABIG's turnaround.

"My focus has always been on people because that's where the money is," said Callahan, reflecting on his career. "My results are always bottom-line/profit-oriented. I couldn't hold a job if I didn't get bottom-line results."

Callahan's results at ABIG—headquartered in South Barrington, Illinois (a Chicago suburb) and one of three operating units of Allstate Insurance Company—speak for themselves. When he assumed leadership, ABIG was losing money and its future was in doubt. Just three years later, despite a heavy financial toll exacted by Florida's Hurricane Andrew, they made a profit. And this when Allstate's personal lines, and other insurance companies, suffered huge losses.

Another evidence of ABIG's transformation was that one of its teams was among 14 finalists in nearly 500 entries to win the 1993 Rochester Institute of Technology and USA TODAY Quality Cup Award. Also in 1993, the company's extraordinary performance resulted in a gainsharing payout of over $9 million.

The Turnaround Story

"When Allstate asked me to head its business insurance unit, they said, 'You're not going to like this assignment,'" recalled Callahan. "Business insurance had never worked well for us. Allstate asked if I would evaluate the business to determine if it could be salvaged or if we should close it down.

"It took about 100 days to make the evaluation. I had learned from past experience that when things aren't working, the problem is invariably the senior staff—the people who have the most to lose. They became successful based on their experiences and see no reason for changing their success pattern.

"So whenever I've been involved in a turnaround situation, I've always looked at my staff immediately. At ABIG, I began by asking everyone the same question: 'If you were going to build a new insurance business across the street, who would you take with you—who are the movers and shakers? I collected hundreds of names and discovered that the same 35 people were on everyone's list. And they were from all levels of the organization.

"I had recognized that, for speed, I couldn't get the job done with the old-fashioned structure. So I immediately removed two layers and had 16 people reporting to me on the senior level. During this initial period, I tried to determine if we had enough talent to bring about transformation and make this company a winner. When I identified the 35, I knew it was more than enough.

"Once we made the decision with Sears and Allstate to take ABIG forward, we asked several of the 35 potential leaders to join our senior officers at an offsite location to develop a vision. You have to set your aspirations high—so high that they capture everyone's imagination and commitment. In the vision we finally arrived at, we agreed that we would be an aggressive, forward-thinking company. Our vision was going to carry us not only into the mid-90's, but into the 21st century.

"We were so audacious that we said we would be a world-class provider of products and services to selected segments of the business insurance marketplace. We would go from being a generalist to serving a niche: small to mid-size businesses.

"People said, 'Are you crazy?' We were not respected at all in our corporate family. They felt we didn't measure up and weren't of the same caliber as other Allstate companies. We accepted that perception, but got on with it. We spent late 1989 bringing in new people, setting up our transformation, and training people.

"Then in January 1990, we announced our new company—a matrix organization that eliminated management layers, de-emphasized hierarchy, and stressed the role of teams at every level. We published a letter spelling out all that we would be doing in the next four to six years. That letter now is published every year or two so that people will know we're living by what we said.

"When we started the process, we began pushing decision making and leadership down into the ranks. The 35 people became the stars of the revolutionary transformation. I rotated them to various parts of the organization—different levels, profit centers, and areas of the country—so they could gain experience. About half of them also received training at universities. And I coached my senior staff constantly and met with each of them three times a year, person to person.

"Meanwhile, once a month, I introduced one of the 18 imperatives from my tool kit. A woman who now is a senior officer was puzzled by this piecemeal approach. She said, 'Jack, if you have a plan, why don't you share it with us?' Well, it wasn't appropriate to share it then. If you let people know there are 18 things that are going to change the way they live, you'll overwhelm them.

"If past was prologue, most of the senior managers would have trouble making the transition to the new organization. I didn't want them to downplay or destroy the 18 imperatives, which was possible if I gave them an overview in advance. I wanted to help them change if they could. My personal bias was that they wouldn't be able to. If you can help them change, however, you've got a tremendous win.

"In introducing the new imperatives, I knew that transformation at this level—whether you're a company of 40,000 people or 4,000, as we were—takes four to six years. You can change quickly—we actually changed in 18 months—but it takes four to six years for the change to become institutionalized, or people will revert back to the old way of doing things.

"Communication was critical. We kept disseminating a steady stream of magazine and newspaper articles and reports on subjects like teamwork, technology and training. We also discussed the same topics in our company publications and videotapes, at meetings, and even in the elevators. It was a matter of letting the change process percolate.

"We were setting the foundation and then going forward. I was looking for critical mass. I'd read that 20 percent of the people are always with you when you take over something new. And I felt I had that support. But I was trying to reach 35% because when you reach that kind of acceptance, you win big.

"I measured the support during my field trips around the country, talking with employees. All of a sudden, I thought we had reached that magical number. We had introduced our 18 imperatives and people were beginning to practice them. We were working in teams, some of which were self-managed. Attitudes were good. The changes were starting to take. And people were beginning to view change not as an obstacle, but as a way of life.

"So in June 1991, just 18 months after we had begun our transformation, our top people gathered for a meeting we called 'The End of the Beginning.' We declared the beginning over and started to move into the more mature company. We began by designing measurements for our 18 imperatives to track our progress.

"And we focused on two new ideas. The first was the importance of velocity—the need for a world-class company to be 'fast, fluid, and flexible.' We said we had to increase the pace of change and the sense of urgency within our organization.

"The second was to go public with the ideas and principles we'd been discussing for the past 18 months and to present them as our Leadership System, built around the Empowered Knowledge Worker."

The Empowered Knowledge Worker

"Everything I'd done was to work toward the Knowledge Worker," continued Callahan. "The world has evolved from harnessing land, to harnessing energy, to the Information Age where the key to the future is harnessing data or knowledge. The great breakthrough in our transformation was the realization that the future belongs to the Knowledge Workers. We recognized that our success depended upon our ability to train the front-line worker—the lawyers, actuaries, underwriters, and sales, marketing and claims people.

"So the challenge was, how can we make the Knowledge Worker

stand tall with knowledge, support, confidence and trust? Not management, but communications was going to do that. For example, today we arm our field people with laptops, cellular phones and faxes. Instead of having to go back to the hotel to telephone vendors about a repair job, they talk to them right on the job. After Hurricane Andrew, 93% of our claim group's customers were very satisfied, 7% were satisfied, and none were dissatisfied.

"But in addition to providing technology, you need to teach your people and provide the education and training. We have 50 hours of mandatory training annually for our employees, whom we now call 'associates.'

"One of our great breakthroughs was an emphasis on profit. We introduced the Great Game of Business concept, a computer-based program. It taught our people about such things as profit and loss, the balance sheet, and how everything they do interacts with others and impacts their jobs.

"As you develop people, a wonderful event occurs. All of a sudden, you're getting that discretionary effort, that voluntary piece. And that's when you take off. Instead of workers coming to work and feeling satisfied with the pay, working conditions and benefits, you get workers who feel good about what's happening. Because we care about them and have proven it over time, they're willing to give us a voluntary performance above and beyond what we expect. It seemed to take forever for that to happen. But when it did, we declared the end of the beginning.

"If you have Knowledge Workers and empower them and give them the tools they need to act independently and then provide strong leadership, you'll win. If you're not empowering people, you're not giving them the right to be responsible. You don't have the right not to empower people, to hold back their training and education.

"Some people say empowerment is nothing more than a fad. It's hard to combat this attitude among people who have the old-fashioned approach to leadership. They don't understand that empowerment means both letting go and taking control. It's a paradox. For example, I receive tremendous packages of data and information about our business. If I see a problem, I'll step in immediately. I'm not going to sit back and hope that the empowered people will change the situation. That's not fair to them, or to the organization and the other associates.

"My job as a leader is to know when to move in and when not to. Say your people are going down a road with curbs on either side. You let them operate within the curbs, but if they go over a curb, you make sure you get them back on the road. That's what I try to do because, ultimately, if I'm not faithful to the bottom line, we won't have a company.

"The final step we took in supporting the Empowered Knowledge Worker was changing the name of our home office group to the Field Support Group. Until then, the perceptions hadn't actually changed. In the past, no matter how good we were at building imperatives in the organization, no matter how well we worked as a team, the field people resented the fact that orders still seemed to be coming down from the home office. Now with the name and behavior change, it's clear that the home group is supporting the field, not directing. it.

"Because I knew I was retiring the following year, I also put in place the last major change in our transformation process. We appointed territorial leaders to represent the field group and the Field Support Group. Associates in the Field Support Group are assigned to a territorial team, as well as doing their own normal functions.

"The territorial leaders report back to me and the senior staff on what is working and what is not and on what I have to protect the groups from. For one, I have to protect them from staff members who may revert back to the old way of doing things when I leave."

18 Imperatives of Success

"At the center of our Leadership System is the individual—the Empowered Knowledge Worker—who is surrounded and supported by 18 essential tools," continued Callahan. "The tools are like gears you engage when you need them. They're not stand-alone, but are linked. Of the 18 imperatives, 11 are processes and seven are environmental conditions. I knew that if we did the processes well, the seven—creativity, innovation, involvement, initiative, diversity, recognition and trust—would occur.

"Two imperatives set our direction. These are vision and leadership. You have to start with a vision that is crisp, clear and simplified so people can understand it and really get behind it. Our vision was to be world class—which means being the very best at what we do. But here's the secret: You never get to your destination, because it's constantly being redefined by the marketplace.

"The second imperative is leadership. What is the difference between leadership and managership? Leaders bring about the change process. Managers are involved with the complexity of the organization. You need managers—your controllers, technology people, etc.—they're critical to the organization. But you need leaders to handle the change process.

"In my career at Allstate, I saw the difference between good and bad leadership. I was transferred a number of times back to the New England Regional Office, but in different jobs. What I discovered was that things that once worked well were no longer working. Why? Because the management had changed.

"I found a correlation between attitude, leadership and the bottom line. For example, if underwriters had a bad attitude or were badly led, their frequency rates—the number of accidents per 100 units—were high. If you had a bad attitude in a claims unit, the severity, or cost per claim, was high. Instead of settling a bodily injury claim in the low-to-mid range, they settled in the mid-to-high. I saw that bad attitudes led to high frequency and high severity.

"If the front-line people who were making critical decisions every day had good attitudes with good leadership, the results were very, very good. When the opposite occurred, the results were very bad. A good attitude is critical to getting the job done, no matter what your work. Seeing the difference between good and bad leadership, I realized that I couldn't afford bad attitudes among my people.

"Another of our 18 imperatives is teams. By 1991, we were working in teams and today about a third of our offices have self-managed teams. We didn't put managers in as team leaders. Instead, we had most of them coaching and facilitating. The teams chose their own leaders. The biggest problem we experienced is that team leaders tended to emulate their past managers. But we didn't want them to do things the old way because the old way never worked. Eventually, people bought into that. We've had many failures and successes and learned much. We think we've mastered teams.

"Communication is another imperative. To insure this, we put in place two feedback devices. One is the opinion survey, which we conduct during the last half of the year, using our personal computers. When we have the results, we choose representatives to talk with management and discuss the concerns and the reasons behind them.

"The second feedback device is our upward communication process, which is critically important. This works better than anything I've ever done. My senior staff and I meet with representative associates. Immediate managers never attend because they might inhibit the associates. And we hold separate upward communications meetings for middle managers anyway. The ground rule is that the associates are not speaking for themselves, but for their peers.

"After these meetings, we consolidate all the concerns, print them, and get them back to the associates. Then we have an action program. After awhile, senior managers may say they don't need to do the upward communications process anymore, that everything has been solved. But the fact is, everything never is. This process is a way to check and also to build the trust of people. The opinion surveys and upward communications are ways to keep people venting. Without that, people will revert back to the old way.

"Technology is another of the imperatives and a tremendous driver for us. We brought in a new person who changed the whole technology concept here. And we assigned top managers in technology to all of our profit centers. In the past, we had integrated technology only in select areas of the business. Also, our systems were not tied into our business plans. They were functional, but didn't speak to each other.

"We lost ten years because we treated technology as an expense, not an investment. Today, we know that the value of technology extends well beyond operation efficiencies. It enables us to discover, gather and process information to reshape the business itself. And it increases our capacity to act.

"Another imperative is diversity. From the beginning of our transformation, we advocated diversity long before it was popular in business. For example, three of our 35 movers and shakers were women and now are officers, something unheard of in the past.

"Diversity is a reality here because people can see it. They see that everyone is equal and has God-given skills and abilities. ABIG must train people and set the tone on top for people to be all they can be."

Lessons Learned

"I found that if I did the processes in my tool kit well, then involvement occurred and this is so critical," said Callahan. "If you get the majority of the people involved in their company as owners and really believe it, they begin to initiate things. I also learned that the biggest thing we can accomplish is to have people stand tall, on their own two feet, and recognize that they've got skill and ability. I've noticed that people with self confidence do a terrific job. My job is to build self confidence.

"Another lesson was that people have to be able to build a skill base and recognize that we don't owe them a living. Collectively, we owe each other a living. We all have to work someplace, and so we might as well make wherever we're working the very best there is. If you get this message across and back it up with programs that work, you'll win.

"If you're going to be a player in the new world of business in the Information Age, you're going to do it only through your people. They've got to be world class to get there. There's no other choice.

You're going to have to invest in all of these processes and achieve the environmental conditions to change behaviors and attitudes.

"If you have knowledgeable people working in teams in the Information Age, and arm them with technology, and take down all the barriers, there's nothing that can hold you back. Once you have empowerment within your company, there's no way in the world you can lose."

* * * * *

The 18 Imperatives

The first two Imperatives set direction:
- *Vision* is the roadmap in decision making, our picture of the future.
- *Leadership* creates the environment that inspires and enables everyone to achieve his or her full potential.

The next three Imperatives lay the foundation:
- *Teams* break barriers and build skills and knowledge; they require commitment, contribution and ownership, enabling empowerment to occur.
- *Organization* is constantly evolving and flexible in response to customers' ever-changing needs and demands for speed and flexibility.
- *Quality* is found in everything we do, to meet and exceed customer expectations.

Three more Imperatives stimulate listening:
- *Communication* is boundaryless—an ongoing, open and honest exchange of ideas and information with customers, agents and other associates.
- *Opinion Surveys* manifest leadership's commitment to listening and responding to issues.
- *Technology* enables us to access and utilize information or knowledge to reshape the business.

The next seven Imperatives create and define the environment:
- *Creativity* is the use of the imagination to create tomorrow, today.

- *Innovation,* an element of continuous improvement, encourages experimentation and risk taking.
- *Involvement* requires full participation and commitment.
- *Initiative* is a "just do it" approach to getting the job done.
- *Diversity* values and maximizes the talents of all.
- *Recognition* is the regular celebration of accomplishment.
- *Trust* is the sum of respect, openness, integrity, performance and communication, and must flow in all directions.

The final three Imperatives support the rest of the system:
- *Education and Training* recognizes that learning is a lifelong process.
- *People Development* is the critical investment in our future—growing of our most important asset.
- *Coaching* is helping people to discover their own capabilities.

Taken together, these 18 Imperatives of Success provide the levers for the transformation of Allstate Business Insurance. They are constants in the midst of pervasive change. They complement and support each other.

Date of Case Study: December, 1994

1997 Epilogue: Shortly after this interview, Jack Callahan retired and Allstate broke the Business Insurance Group into smaller components. Three of them were sold in 1996 after the company made a strategic decision to focus on its core business, personal lines insurance.

Callahan said, "If we hadn't rehabilitated the group, it would have been closed in 1990, many people would have lost their jobs, and Allstate wouldn't have had profitable businesses to sell today—above their book value, I might add. And the people are being treated well. I feel very good about it."

Callahan's experiences have since been further documented in two books: *Leading People,* by Robert H. Rosen, and *Strategies and*

Leadership, by J. Fred McLimore. He now heads the consulting firm, The Callahan Group, Inc., in Deerfield, Illinois.

Part Four

Empowering Employees to Satisfy Customers, Solve Problems and Improve Processes —6 Case Studies

"Never tell people how to do things. Tell them what you want them to do and they will surprise you with their ingenuity."
—Gen. George S. Patton, Jr.

15

Empowerment Through Technology at USAA

PROFILE

Organization: United Services Automobile Association (USAA), a worldwide insurance and diversified financial services institution.
History: Founded in 1922 by 25 U.S. Army officers when other insurers found them too mobile and living too much at risk to qualify for insurance.
Members/Owners and Associates: More than 2.3 million active, retired and former military officers; their dependents are associate members.
Products: A full-range of insurance and financial products and additional services, including the USAA Federal Savings Bank, travel agency, member buying service, 23-story retirement community, and health-care facility.
Employees: 14,000, 64% of them women.
Location: 286-acre headquarters in San Antonio, Texas. Additional offices in Sacramento, California; Colorado Springs, Colorado; Tampa, Florida; Norfolk, Virginia; London, England; and Frankfurt, Germany.
Assets: Owns and manages over $25 billion in assets.
Awards and Recognitions: Site-visited in 1989 and 1990 by Malcolm Baldrige National Quality Award evaluation teams; recipient of 1991 QPMA Leadership Award.

* * * * *

A retired U.S. Air Force brigadier general and former dean of the U.S. Air Force Academy, Robert F. McDermott, CEO of USAA, knows the importance of strategy in winning on the battlefield and in the marketplace. But when he first came to USAA in 1969 and saw the quality of service being offered, he wondered if any strategy could win the battle.

Though the company was good on claims and price and was honest, if fell short in most other categories. And like most insurance companies then, it was drowning in a tidal wave of paper—files, claim forms, applications and correspondence.

USAA was constantly receiving letters and phone calls about its poor service. And because so many of the insurance documents were being lost, McDermott had to hire 200-300 college students to work nights just to search for them on employees' desks. Only USAA's low premiums and good delivery on claims kept members loyal.

McDermott vowed then and there to pursue his "impossible dream" to one day make USAA a "paperless" business. His strategic weapon would be information technology.

It's not surprising, then, that in the past 23 years USAA has been a leader in using the latest technology to improve customer service, and, to make employees' jobs more meaningful. The company has installed everything from an automated policy writing system, to the world's largest automatic call distribution system.

And this strategy has helped the company become the nation's fifth-largest insurer of private automobiles and fourth largest insurer of homes, and, since 1985, to increase its assets by 230%.

But USAA's newest technological weapon—an Automated Insurance Environment With Imaging Plus—is finally making McDermott's dream a reality. Installed in 1988 after years of planning and testing in partnership with IBM, imaging has totally changed the way USAA does business. It has reduced a process that once required 55 separate steps, to just a five-minute phone call. And it has eliminated tons of paper, the need for filing time and storage space, with savings to the company of $5 million annually.

This new technology has brought USAA the improved customer

service and satisfaction it was aiming for. But imaging also has given USAA an unexpected bonus—an effective new way to empower its people.

Gerald L. Gass, director of quality measurement and improvement, Jack Church, policy service area manager, Southwest Texas, and Juana Rodriguez, senior service representative, talked about how the new technology is empowering managers, employees, and members.

Freeing Up Employees

"We're the world's largest user of imaging and that's ironic, because 20 years ago we were talking about being paperless," said Gass. "We see imaging and technology in general as a means of empowering our employees, because it's freeing them to deal with our members.

"It's also enlarged the employees' jobs, because when a call comes in the next day, or the next hour, or the next month, service representatives know exactly what's been done with that member's account and can respond without having to be brought up to speed.

"Imaging has also taken thousands and thousands of files off the floor and put them in a scannable device that's accessible to everyone, not just in San Antonio, but coast to coast."

Seeing the "Real" Thing

The largest direct-mail company in the U.S. in mail-order sales volume, USAA receives about 150,000 pieces of mail daily. With the electronic imaging system, less than half the mail, except for checks, never leaves the mailroom.

Instead, an exact image of the correspondence is indexed and scanned electronically into the member's policy service file in the computer system. This information becomes instantly available anywhere in the company.

At the same time, it's placed in an electronic in-basket, where it's categorized and prioritized. Then, managers assign it to a service representative (SR), identified by employee number, for processing.

In addition to incoming mail, internal work is also brought into the system. For example, if a member's policy needs to be renewed, a renewal worksheet will be put into the system for processing.

All of the SRs have access to the imaging system without leaving their desks. Each work station has two monitors, one for accessing the computer data base, and the other for viewing the actual documents and letters in the imaging system.

Besides expediting the mail, imaging also lets the SR complete transactions over the phone almost instantly. Whenever she—most SRs are women—takes a member's phone call, she can bring up on her terminal any of the member's records. And she can call up on the imaging screen the exact letters or documents in the member's file, even those from years ago.

How the System Works

"The Property and Casualty Policy Service and Underwriting Division was the first to use the new technology," said Church. "About 75% of our business is telephone calls—the rest is incoming mail and internally generated work. Our district alone receives about 3,000 calls a day and, with the new system, the average call takes about four or five minutes. The time varies with the complexity of the policy.

"Our SRs are trained in all lines of vehicle, homeowners and property insurance, so they're able to answer most questions. When they're not busy taking calls, they bring up mail on the imaging system to process.

"When a call comes in, the SR asks for the member's number or name, and uses it to call up on the computer screen the member's policy information. The member's file shows any calls he's made or any correspondence sent from him or generated by USAA. It will also show which SR has worked on the account, what was done and when.

"It also shows all the mail imaged for a member, and when it was imaged. So, if there is a transaction, or if the member is questioning anything, the SR has everything before her.

"If the member says he wants to talk about his auto insurance, the SR can call up on the computer screen the particular coverages the member has and all the premiums for the vehicle. If the member wants to talk about his homeowners' policy, the SR can call up all the information on that.

"Then, she can call up the actual documents and input any changes—add a car, delete a car, change the homeowners coverage. When the transaction is completed, she uses a documentation screen to document briefly what took place.

"If she needs to correspond with a member, she calls up a standard business letter on the screen. Then she selects the applicable paragraph, inputs the member's number, and the system produces the letter and even sends it for her.

"The manager can call up a screen that breaks down the mail—giving the member number, the exact day it was received, the line of business, the kind of transaction, such as special handling, renewal, fire referral and the priority number, which means it requires faster handling. We can see right away which is the most important mail to process.

"A holdover display on the system lets us know how many pieces of mail are in the system to be processed by our area, what line of business, and how old it is. For example, the screen might say we have 1,100 pieces of mail to be processed—360 auto, 140 fire and the rest homeowners.

"After the mail is in the imaging system, managers assign the work to SR's according to their ability and experience. Then, when an SR is ready to work on mail, she simply inputs SW (send work), and the computer sends, by priority, only what the manager has authorized. If an SR has a question about procedures she can call these up on the screen.

"The imaging system gives us a good audit trail," continued Church. "Under the old system, things would fall through the cracks. With this system, we have a trail showing us everyone who's looked at the piece of mail. If something doesn't get handled, we know exactly who didn't do it, and we know the time lapse."

Simple to Use/No Paper

"The imaging system is great because it's easy to use and requires only a few hours of training," continued Church. "It was developed by employees in a 'living lab.' They tested it three or four years before it was brought to us. Everyone's comfortable with it, and the beauty is, there's no paper.

"When I first started working here 15 years ago, everything was manual. It could take two or three days just to mail out a policy, provided there was no backlog. Now, the process time takes a couple of minutes.

"Someone can call in to add a vehicle to his auto policy, and while the SR is talking to the individual, she's keying the information into the system. As soon as the caller hangs up the phone, he has the coverage. At night, everything keyed-in during the day is processed and sent to the communications center to be mailed in the morning."

Empowering Managers and Employees

"The imaging system has changed my job as a manager because it's given me a lot more control," said Church. "Before we had the system, we were managing by the seat of our pants. We had to count stacks of holdover work to know what still had to be done. Now, we have a lot more information and know exactly what work there is at any time.

"We can also control how work is assigned—to whom, what type of business and when. And we can monitor the calls to see how our SRs are handling them.

"The employees are empowered because they have more control over their work. With the old system, the managers would put work on the SRs desks. Now, SRs receive work through the system and call it up when they're ready to work on it. This way, they're managing their own time and working at their own speed, rather than at the speed we dictate.

"And they're motivated to do a good job. If you let people work on their own, they take pride in what they're doing. They're also empowered because they can make more decisions about transactions," continued Church, "so, it's a happy marriage.

"We have limitations on what we trust employees with, depending upon their experience and ability. For example, some SRs can approve a homeowners policy of up to $300,000. Above that amount they need the approval of a senior SR, who also has another higher limit, or a manager.

"Our employees also have been empowered through our PRIDE program, in which they've received training and learned to work on teams to improve processes.

"Our district has four units, each with about 20 employees. The units used to be involved in petty competitions against each other for such things as the highest number of phone calls completed. Each unit was independently trying to come up with better ways of doing things.

"Then, a PRIDE team of two employees from each unit was formed, and they said, 'Why not see if we can give better service to members in the district and not just the unit?'"

A More Efficient Approach

Said Juana Rodriguez, senior service representative, "The new system lets us be much more efficient. A member might call and ask about something he sent us a year ago. In the past, we had to put him on hold and search our file bins for his file, then walk back to our desk, work the file and look for the paper we needed. Now, it's a matter of seconds to find what we need. We just look through our image file, and the document is immediately available on our screen.

"The members are very impressed when we can look at something from a year ago in a matter of seconds.

"We're also empowered because we have a lot more control over our work. If management has given me ten pieces of mail and I can't work on an item because I'm waiting for a call back, I have the power to save it for another day.

"There's also more accountability now and no more phantom SR. We used to be afraid that if a piece of mail came in that was too complex, and the SR might not want to work on it, they might trash it. Now we know exactly when it got to our building, when it was scanned and who worked on it. If later we find that some policy was issued incorrectly, we can backtrack and see who did it. We do this not to point a finger at them, but as a training tool so it won't happen again.

"We're also empowered by limits of authority we've been given to authorize a transaction. If the transaction is beyond the initial SR's limit of authority, that person has the power to at least recommend what should be done."

Expanding to Other Areas

Currently, USAA is working to bring imaging to its claims division and is also working with IBM to develop a multi-media system that includes imaging, pictures, voice and video.

USAA is not interested in technology for its own sake, however. They've invested $130 million in their system because it's the best strategy for providing better service for USAA members, and more satisfying jobs for its employees.

Date of Case Study: July, 1992

1997 Epilogue: "There's been a quite a bit of updating on our imaging system since the article was written four and one-half years ago," said Jack Church. "One of the biggest changes is that a lot of our work now comes in and goes out by fax—right from the system, instead of fax machines. A lot of our members fax things to us from their PCs, and we're able to respond in the same manner. This saves a lot of scanning and overnight entry to the system, and allows us, for example, to literally pull up a copy of a document on the imaging system that a member has lost and fax it to him from our computer terminal in just a couple of minutes instead of the half hour it was taking. Such changes are helping us to be even more responsive to our USAA members.

"The technology has enabled us to give our service representatives much more power. They're now called insurance specialists and are paid on a merit system. They're able to make more decisions on the spot and issue policies in a couple of hours instead of a couple of days. In addition, we've done some reengineering which has resulted in 10-person teams rather than 18- to 20-person units. Now, managers function more like team leaders and do a lot more coaching and counseling. We have a lot more time to spend with our people, which allows us to learn more about their capabilities. And we have the power to empower people when they're ready for it.

"The PRIDE program is alive and well. Our people are hard at work on projects that relate to USAA's key results areas—improve financial strength, service to our members, physical layout, facilities, etc."

16

Winning the War on Cycle Time at Motorola

There was a time when all it took to satisfy customers was a quality product at the right price. But no longer. Now, to succeed in today's fiercely competitive global market, companies have to be able to follow up with excellent after-market support and repair services.

With its Six Sigma goal, Motorola's Cellular Infrastructure Group (CIG) in Arlington Heights, Illinois (a suburb of Chicago) was confident it was producing the highest quality products. But when customers began complaining about service and repairs, Motorola's CIG knew it was in trouble.

At the CIG repair facility, located in Farmers Branch, Texas, repairs were taking as long as 60 days, and repair orders were backed up. Some parts were not available and, as a consequence, customers weren't receiving their orders on time.

Realizing something had to be done immediately, Motorola announced on February 12, 1991, that it was moving the CIG repair facility to its headquarters in Itasca, Illinois. At the same time, CIG employees formed the Higgins' Heroes Total Customer Satisfaction (TCS) team (named for Scott Higgins, operations manager) and declared war on the repair department's cycle time.

Within six months, the team completed the move to Itasca. By the end of 1992, they had reduced the cycle time from 60 days to 5 days, improved the service level to 95%, and reduced costs substantially.

For their outstanding achievement, they received a Silver Award in Motorola's 1992 annual worldwide TCS Competition. In addition, they were honored with a first-time-ever Breadth of Application Award for encompassing the most Motorola functional areas in their project.

CIG managers and Higgins' Heroes talked about their war against cycle time.

One-stop Shop Speeds Up Process

"CIG is responsible for worldwide customer service for our infrastructure products, which are cellular products," explained Debbie Wong, quality analyst, Strategic Quality, and CIG TCS Coordinator. "These include base stations and switches and OEM products we supply to customers.

"CIG participated in the TCS competition for the first time in 1992 and had more than 75 teams. Of our 4,600 employees, 13% were on teams in 1992. [40% of all Motorola employees participated on TCS teams.] The Higgins' Heroes team was the CIG representative in Motorola's corporate-wide competition.

"At Itasca, we have 130 people and call our group After Market Support and Ancillary Products. The one-stop shop is something we developed to make service easy for our customers.

"We supply all OEM products that are sold with Motorola's products. We consolidate equipment from our manufacturing group with equipment from OEM suppliers. Then we ship it to the customer so they receive a complete package. If they need service, they have only one phone number to call."

Fix the Problem, or Lose Customers

Said Cindy Patterson, after market support manager and Higgins' Heroes team leader, "We formed a team not just to participate in the TCS competition, but because our customers were extremely dissatisfied with our service level. In the past, CIG had unsuccessfully contracted out repair service to two other Motorola groups.

"CIG said 'It looks like we're going to have to pick this up ourselves to make sure service levels are where we need them.' We had two choices: we could either fix the problem, or lose customers.

"When people buy things today, they're not just interested in the product. They also want to know what service they're going to get after they've purchased it. Because service is so much more important now, we needed to fix ours. If we didn't, we might not sell any new products."

Attacking with a Cross-functional Team

Continued Wong, "A lot of teams are often from a single department. This team stood out because it was cross-functional. Besides Itasca, it included people from all over Motorola. Higgins' Heroes chose 12 people to make the TCS presentation and represent their success, but many more worked behind the scenes."

Explained Tim Anstead, customer satisfaction supervisor, "To identify the problem areas, each group submitted items they wanted to address. Then we created a fish bone diagram listing problems that were reasons for customer dissatisfaction. Next, we targeted key points to fix that which would give us the most results."

Recalled Patterson, "We benchmarked with our suppliers to learn the industry standard. They had a ten-day cycle time, little backlog, and about a 70% service level, with few delinquencies.

"And we also benchmarked with our major customers, who were the people judging us. They had higher expectations and wanted a five-day cycle time. Obviously, they wanted no backlog or delinquencies. And some wanted to be able to call and get the parts shipped the same day.

"Based on our benchmarking, we developed a mission statement for our entire organization. To provide 'Best in Class' customer service, we needed immediate response time, a 5-day repair cycle time, next-day delivery on new part sales, and continuous follow-up. Later, because of customer feedback, we revised the statement to say we'll deliver new products when the customer wants them."

Driving Cycle Time Down

"The repair business is very unpredictable," said Mohammad Akhtar, lead engineer. "We repair and test eight different product lines, both analog and digital. We can get one type one day, and a different type the next. So, to reduce the cycle time, we cross-trained all our technicians to be able to work on two or more products."

Added Patti Modzelewski, business planner, "We also designed a shipping label to make the receiving process quicker. We were having problems with things getting shipped to the wrong Motorola facility. We decided that if we gave customers a nice bright label with our address, it would expedite the delivery to us.

"Once the part got here, the label speeded up receiving because the customer referenced the return material authorization number. So, we knew exactly who the unit belonged to."

Said Akhtar, "Our engineers and technicians also developed a summarized list of common equipment defects, based on history. We put the list on the tag, and now customers just circle the problem. If it isn't listed, they describe it briefly. So, the list makes it easier to troubleshoot."

Added John Stipek, repair technician, "When no trouble is found, we call the customer personally to find out exactly what they're experiencing. Then we try to simulate the problem. We've made the phone call a mandatory part of the process. You can't send a board back without resolution."

Added Bradley Wheeler, repair technician, "Many times when I've called a customer, the board they sent wasn't the problem. They needed to know this so they wouldn't pull certain modules from their system."

Said Debbie Ramunno, customer service representative, "We don't have any qualms about having technicians talk to customers.

We make a lot of conference calls to try to resolve issues over the phone."

Said Patterson, "We've also developed standard definitions for certain repairs. That way, we don't have different descriptions for the same problem. And because we have different types of service, another thing that made a big difference was color-coded tags. Customers can request repair and return on their own module, or they can request a pre-exchange, in which we exchange a good board for their defective one.

"We were having trouble identifying for our technicians which boards customers were waiting for. Now everything gets tagged when it comes in. Any board with a red tag is customer-owned and takes priority over everything else.

"We also developed a quality report that the customer receives with every repair. It shows what parts we replaced and why, and includes test results and our cycle time from the date we received the part until we shipped it."

Advantages of a New Facility

"One advantage of our new facility," continued Patterson, "was that two of our people, Mohammad Akhtar and Sam Valenti from Facilities, designed its layout."

Explained Valenti, "We have domestic and international products, and also some products that have been canceled, but which we're required to support in accordance with contracts. We kept two things in mind in designing the layout: the flow through the repair center, and the difference in the frequencies for international and domestic products. If they're next to each other, there can be interference problems. So, we kept those sections separated."

Said Patterson, "Another helpful thing is that Customer Service (CS) is located with the repair center. In Texas, CS was clear across the building.

"Having our manufacturing facility nearby is also important. In field repair operations, you need support from Development

Engineering and Manufacturing Engineering. And you need to feed back defects to the engineering group so they can design better in the future. In the past, our engineers couldn't fly to Texas for every problem. Now, Itasca is just a 15-minute drive."

Database Tracks Failures

Explained Darin Hall, Quality Assurance, "We put together a database to track all the information as units came in and were repaired. We can sort failures by customer, or by area. For example, by tracking failures by region, we saw that the southeastern U.S.. was having a lot of lightning problems. Knowing this helped us in that area.

"We also can track failures down to components. Components Engineering uses the data to see if there are components across different products that are showing high failure rates."

Added Stipek, "When we find root cause problems in components, we can track them to the vendor. We feed back the information about the problem, and whether the vendor has made the adjustment or if we need to qualify another vendor. We demand Six Sigma [near perfection] of our vendors, as well as of ourselves."

Continued Hall, "We also can compare customer failure rates with those of other customers to see if they're above or below the standard failure rate for a certain part. If they're above, that's a red flag to the customer rep. The rep will work with engineering to help the customer determine why they're having higher failures. Our responsibility is not just to fix the product, but to help the customers prevent failures."

Keys to Achieving Goals

Said Patterson, "One key to our success was that we had a very structured schedule, with a list of tasks, the people responsible, and the date the action had to be completed. We also had daily meetings to learn the status of each unit to be repaired. Representatives from all the functions attended the meetings, which we still hold daily.

"Another key to success was documenting all the procedures and implementing processes. We developed two procedures books—one for the repair center and one for Customer Service."

Added Earl Casas, customer service representative, "In handling accounts, we thought it might be difficult for customers if they had to speak to different people whenever they called. We assigned a customer representative and an alternate to each customer so they're familiar with the customer's history and needs."

Said Anstead, "Another obstacle was that many customers don't speak English. It was very difficult for them to convey the problems they were having. Interpreters would try, but something was frequently lost. So, we hired Customer Service Representatives who are able to interface with customers in their native language."

Said Modzelewski, "We also extended our service hours from 7 a.m. to 7 p.m. so we're working when our customers are. This satisfies our customers no matter what time zone they're in. Our reps have flexible hours and come in very early or stay late, or even take phone calls at home so they can stay in contact with their customers."

Said Anstead, "We had a phone system that couldn't track our calls. For a while, we were even running on two phone systems. So we implemented a new system that gives us all the tracking we need and more. We can personalize toll-free numbers that target specific announcements to customers. And we can give international customers their own phone number so they'll get recorded announcements in their native language."

Said Alan Zindler, financial analyst, "The repair facility had never been managed as its own profit-and-loss center until it was moved here. We've put in a business management system and have had more business, with better pricing and closer monitoring of costs. We also offer service contracts to customers when they're out of warranty."

Customers Monitor Cycle Times

Continued Patterson, "We didn't want to disillusion ourselves about our cycle time, so we asked some customers to monitor us. When we were putting in our management system, the cycle time started to creep up for one customer. I was on the phone to them right away, wanting to know what was happening because our internal cycle time wasn't increasing. They explained that they had changed to a cheaper, but slower, carrier. Our cycle time was fine with them."

Said Anstead, "We're now implementing a Customer Care Program, including customer surveys and follow-up calls."

Added Patterson, "Currently we're working on our international cycle time. We're trying to take ownership for the entire cycle time, from when the customer ships it until they have it back again. Some countries make it impossible to reduce the cycle time because of customs delays. So we've established Rotopool Sites in those countries.

"Our first Rotopool opened in June in China, currently our biggest international customer. The Rotopool rotates parts; we supply the customer with a working unit and the defective board is sent to the U.S. repair."

How They Won the War

"It's important to have cross-functional representation," said Zindler. "We had a lot of people from different experiences who all focused on the same thing."

Said Patterson, "Early in the transition, we had no ground rules. Everybody was expected to do anything. We had management unpacking boxes and packing people making management decisions. We just let the group take its natural course—whoever had the best idea."

Said Wheeler, "There was a lot of pressure, but then someone would break the ice with a joke. We had fun, but we knew we had work to get back to."

Operations Manager Scott Higgins summarized, "You have to

have a willingness to do this kind of teamwork. Everyone on the team had a desire to succeed, to support our customers. A passion to succeed. And it's catching. It starts with the team leader and filters down.

"You also need the ability to let go. If the team failed, they would try another approach. In the case of Higgins' Heroes, they succeeded tremendously. There's no magic formula; it has a lot to do with attitude—do you want to succeed?"

Date of Case Study: July, 1993

1997 Epilogue: Tom Maher, Operations Manager for Motorola's Worldwide Cellular Services reports that the repair facility is managing to maintain its exemplary performance in cycle time and customer service for its domestic work, despite a substantial increase in business.

"Since the efforts put forth by the Higgins' Heroes Total Customer Satisfaction Team, there has been significant growth in the customer service business," he said. "The customer base has increased by approximately 70%, the number of countries supported has increased by roughly 150% and the operation has become truly global.

"Many of the tools and ideas originally implemented by Higgins' Heroes have had to be modified in support of this phenomenal growth. As each new challenge is identified, an appropriate cross-functional team is formed to identify solutions. There are numerous Total Customer Satisfaction teams currently working on new customer service challenges.

"For example, one team has recently been formed to work with customers to further minimize delays in shipping and customs. As always, identifying and then meeting or exceeding measurable goals and cost objectives are part of the process. These teams exist long enough to complete a project, insure that it's implemented and performing as expected. Once this occurs, the teams dissolve, and the members create new teams with new personnel to work on new challenges.

"This process of constant renewal allows customers to continually receive better service while the team members continue to learn transferable skills that will help them throughout their careers at Motorola."

17

Reducing Turnaround Time at SwedishAmerican Hospital

Debra G. French, Development Specialist &
Katherine L. Hermansen, Manager, Management Engineering

Over the years, the Laboratory at SwedishAmerican Hospital has received many complaints about excessively long turnaround times for arterial blood gas (ABG) tests ordered in the Intensive and Coronary Care Units. The Hospital formed a team to improve the process using the Juran Quality Improvement Methodology.

A comparison of turnaround time to customer expectations revealed that average turnaround time under the existing system was acceptable to only 4% of the customers. Detailed flow diagrams, a cause and effect diagram, and data allowed the team to determine the causes of the lengthy turnaround time. Brainstorming techniques identified potential solutions which were reviewed for feasibility, ease of implementation, and financial viability.

A remedy consisting of work and job redesign led to a 71% reduction in turnaround time. This improved turnaround time meets the expectations of more than 90% of surveyed customers — proving that Total Quality Management methodology can be successfully employed to solve problems in the clinical setting.

Background

SwedishAmerican Hospital is a 397-bed acute care hospital in Rockford, Illinois, serving northern Illinois and southern Wisconsin. Its services include cardiovascular medicine, oncology, pediatric intensive care, emergency medicine, and mental health.

Turnaround time for arterial blood gases (ABGs) in the Intensive and Coronary Care Units (ICCU) has been a recurring problem for caregivers at SwedishAmerican for many years. Over the years, this problem has been extensively studied with no significant changes in performance.

An ABG is a diagnostic laboratory test that measures the amount of oxygen in the blood. There are three types of ABG: stat, routine, and timed. These different types of ABG differ as to the way in which they are ordered. For example, a stat ABG is ordered to be drawn immediately, a timed ABG is ordered to be drawn at a specific time, and a routine ABG is ordered to be drawn during a general time period. The blood specimens that are necessary to perform an ABG are obtained in two ways. They are drawn from an arterial line or from an artery via a puncture.

SwedishAmerican's desire to provide cost efficient quality health care led to its commitment to the TQM philosophy. Educational opportunities on the subject of TQM were first offered to officers and upper management. Individuals throughout the organization were then selected to be educated on facilitation skills and the quality improvement tools at the Juran Institute. Three pilot projects were then selected to introduce the TQM techniques throughout the organization.

One of these pilot projects addressed the problem of "consistently unacceptable turnaround times for arterial blood gases in ICCU." The quality improvement team formed to solve this problem was a multi-disciplinary, cross-departmental team with representation from Respiratory Therapy, ICCU, Nursing, Management Engineering, and the Laboratory. The team's mission was to "achieve an acceptable turnaround time for arterial blood gases drawn in the ICCU."

The team members received four hours of formal training by the team's facilitator prior to starting the project. Additional training was conducted by the team's facilitator and management engineering member on a "just in time" basis.

Diagnostic Journey

The team first determined the percentage of ABGs ordered by type. The data showed that the majority of all ABGs drawn in ICCU were timed ABGs. As a result, the team focused its efforts on improving the turnaround time for timed ABGs. This decision was made with the assumption that any solutions that reduced turnaround time for timed ABGs would also reduce turnaround time for stat and routine ABGs. The mission statement was revised as follows: "to achieve an acceptable turnaround time for timed arterial blood gases drawn in the ICCU."

The team believed that it was very important to address customer needs. The value of any improvement in turnaround time was dependent upon how well it met customer needs. Physicians, ICCU nurses, and respiratory therapists were surveyed to determine their expectations for turnaround times of timed ABGs. These customers were asked to identify their "ideal" and "minimally acceptable" turnaround times. The survey results showed that 100% of those surveyed wanted their timed ABG results in 30 minutes or less.

After customer needs had been assessed, the team collected data to determine if these needs were being met by the existing system. The team knew that turnaround time was a problem, given the anecdotal evidence that existed, but did not know the extent of the problem. The team constructed a high-level flow diagram to increase its familiarity with the process and to identify data collection points. The objectives of data collection were: 1) to determine turnaround time for timed ABGs and the average time for each segment of the process and, 2) to determine if turnaround time varied by shift, by draw type, or by person drawing the specimen. Data were collected in the ICCU and Laboratory over a two week period.

Data collection revealed that the process was highly variable. Turnaround times ranged from under 20 minutes to over 140 minutes with an average of 51 minutes. A comparison of actual turnaround times to customer expectations showed that existing turnaround times only met the expectations of 4% of the customers. This finding clearly presented an opportunity for improvement.

The data also showed that no single segment of the process was responsible for the lengthy turnaround times. Each segment of the process contributed to the turnaround time problem. Stratifying the data by hour of day revealed that turnaround times were longer in the early morning hours (e.g., 6 a.m. - 9 a.m.) and during lunch hours (e.g. 12 p.m. - 1 p.m.). Stratification also showed that turnaround time varied by draw type. An ABG drawn via an arterial line had a significantly shorter turnaround time than an ABG drawn via a puncture. In addition, stratification showed that turnaround time varied depending on who drew the specimen. When an arterial specimen was drawn by a phlebotomist, turnaround time was approximately 15 minutes longer than when the specimen was drawn by a nurse or respiratory therapist.

Detailed flow diagrams for the process were constructed. The team found that the ABG process was very lengthy and complicated and varied by shift and by person. The flow diagram for the ABG process filled 13 pages.

The team then conducted brainstorming sessions to identify theories for causes of lengthy turnaround times. These causes were then organized into a Cause and Effect Diagram. The Cause and Effect Table for this information follows:

Delays in Ordering
- Incorrect order
- Lack of patient number
- Last comment on ACTION erases all other comments
- Computer interface delay
- Incorrect procedure
- A.M. draw clipboard is incorrect
- Unnecessary phone use
- Ordering procedures differ by shift

- Test not ordered in a timely manner
- Order not received by clerk
- Order not flagged
- MD holds onto chart
- Computer down
- RN not notified of need by MD
- Shortage or unavailability of clerical staff
- Chart in wrong place

Delays in Collection
- Inability to obtain arterial sample
- Unsuccessful puncture
- Inability to find RN for line draw
- No procedure identifying who is to draw
- Patient care procedures conflict with draw time
- Labels lost
- Computer malfunction
- Printer ran out of labels
- Labels fell off tray
- Labels stuck together
- Lack of timely response by phlebotomists
- Phlebotomists in other areas
- Lack of person for ICCU
- Insufficient number of phlebotomists
- Inability to prioritize multiple orders
- Incomplete information
- ACTION comment not entered or not written
- No protocol for prioritizing
- Lack of communication between ICCU and Lab
- A.M. draw clipboard is inaccurate
- Inconsistent methods between shifts

Delays in Analysis
- Inability to find Med Tech
- Open positions
- Doing phlebotomy
- Running other tests
- In other departments
- Inability to prioritize multiple orders
- Incomplete information
- No protocols for prioritizing
- Clerk busy
- ACTION comment erased/not written

Delays in Reporting
- Computer interface delayed/down
- Incomplete order
- Failure to verify and enter results
- Failure to follow protocol for questionable results
- Tech on phone
- Tech busy elsewhere
- Shortage of staff
- Inability to enter results
- Computer down
- Lack of patient LN number

Delays in Transport
- STAT in other areas
- Multiple ABGs at once
- Distance of ABG machine to ICCU

After reviewing the data, flow diagrams, and cause and effect diagram, the team reasoned that delays in the ordering, collection, analysis, reporting, and transport segments of the process resulted in unacceptably long turnaround times. The team also believed that long turnaround times were due to the highly variable process, inconsistencies across shifts and staff, and a lack of accountability. As a result, the team's objective was to develop solutions to minimize and/or eliminate delays, reduce variability, and increase consistency and accountability.

Remedial Journey

As previously discussed, several root causes were discovered. The team brainstormed to identify remedies to remove these causes. This brainstorming resulted in twenty-five potential remedies to remove the causes for increased turnaround time (TAT). Four potential remedies were selected for testing based on their ability to provide the most significant decreases in turnaround time. Each remedy was explored to determine its effect on turnaround time using pilot studies and cost/benefit analysis. Ease of implementation was also considered. Return on investment analyses were not conducted as the service of providing arterial blood gases was not a new service. As a result, there would be no increase in revenue, only a potential increase in expense.

The four remedies that were studied included point of care testing, STAT lab within the Laboratory, equipment upgrade, and work and job redesign using a pneumatic tube system. After an extensive analysis, the team selected the remedy of work and job redesign. Prior to selecting this remedy, the team conducted a pilot study and measured the TAT at four different points in the process. The data revealed that work and job redesign led to a significant decrease in turnaround time. This decrease occurred without adding staff or purchasing capital equipment.

The selected remedy involved fourteen design changes. The following five changes had the largest impact on TAT:
- ICCU registered nurses and respiratory therapists will draw the arterial blood specimens instead of phlebotomists

- Specimens will be transported from ICCU to the Laboratory through a pneumatic tube system rather than being hand carried
- Physicians will stagger ABG ordering times
- Physicians will use arterial lines for patients requiring multiple draws as feasible
- A special morning phlebotomy team will draw blood specimens throughout the hospital (except ICCU) so that the medical technologists can stay in the Laboratory and run the ABG tests as soon as the blood specimens are received.

Implementation of the design change that required the ICCU nurses to draw the arterial blood specimens was met with resistance. At first, this change was viewed unfavorably by the nurses who saw it as an additional duty to their already heavy work load. Education and communication were used by the team to overcome the nurses' resistance. The nurses bought into the change after they realized that drawing the arterial specimens provided them with more control over their patients' care.

Holding the Gains

Following implementation, data were collected to determine if the solutions had impacted turnaround time. The data revealed that average turnaround time had decreased by 61% from 51 minutes to 20 minutes. This decrease was made possible by improvements in each segment of the process.

A turnaround time of 20 minutes will meet the expectations of 84% of the customers surveyed. Improved turnaround times will benefit many customers. Nurses and respiratory therapists will have more control over their patients' care. Physicians will be able to make patient care decisions in a more timely manner. Medical technologists should experience increased job satisfaction as they are performing medical technology duties rather than phlebotomy duties.

The team's solutions have eliminated the batch arrivals of specimens in the Laboratory, reduced transport delays, and leveled the Laboratory's workload. In addition, the solutions have streamlined the process and reduced process variability. The ABG process is now consistent across shifts and staff. In addition, the solutions have increased accountability. Another benefit of these solutions is that they relied on work and job redesign to reduce turnaround time, rather than relying on a capital purchase. The hospital had budgeted more than $100,000 for equipment that now was not needed due to the team's solutions.

Data collection has shown that the original gains have been expanded. Turnaround time now averages 15 minutes—a 71% reduction from the original turnaround time. This meets more than 90% of customer expectations. In addition, process variability has continued to decline with the majority of ABG turnaround times taking less than 10 minutes.

Monitoring is required to hold the gains that have been achieved by the remedy. On a daily basis, the Chemistry supervisor generates a turnaround time report from the Laboratory's information system. Turnaround times are then reviewed, and outliers are investigated.

The success of these solutions was studied by another quality improvement team at SwedishAmerican. A team chartered to reduce turnaround time for lab tests in the Emergency Department (E.D.) has followed the ABG Team's lead and has recommended that E.D. nurses draw specimens in an effort to reduce turnaround time.

This quality improvement team was recognized by the Rochester Institute of Technology and USA Today as a leader in quality improvement with the 1993 Quality Cup Award in the not-for-profit division. The Quality Cup is presented to teams who make significant contributions to the improvement of quality products and services in an organization.

Lessons Learned

The members of this quality improvement pilot project team, along with the administrators of SwedishAmerican Hospital, learned many lessons during this project. First, and foremost, the QI Project Selection Committee learned that they must assure that data are available to confirm the existence and extent of a problem before chartering a team. The ABG Team spent many months determining if there was a quality improvement opportunity since the team was chartered based on subjective, informal complaints and concerns regarding ABG turnaround time.

Secondly, the team learned that it is imperative to identify and assess customer needs and measure how adequately those needs are being met. Thirdly, the team learned the importance of proper team membership. It became obvious during the flow diagramming process that some of the key people who actually carried out the process hadn't been originally included as team members. Not having the appropriate team members from the outset of the project delayed the team's progress and could have led to the identification of the wrong root cause(s) or remedy.

In addition, this team learned the importance of creating a non-threatening environment for the team to function within. The team members were, at first, hesitant to "tell the truth" about how the process "really was." As a result, the first set of flow diagrams was developed as the process was supposed to be, not as it actually was being operationalized.

Lastly, the team learned to *never* underestimate a human being's inherent resistance to change. This team implemented many changes —both large and small. Resistance to change occurred in all cases —even when the change decreased a person's work load or increased their job satisfaction. Because resistance to change was such a huge issue, the team spent a large amount of time addressing resistance as the remedies were implemented.

Conclusion

The changes to the ABG process were implemented from October 1992 to February 1993 by ICCU, Respiratory Therapy, and the Laboratory with the guidance of the quality improvement team. As mentioned earlier, ongoing monitoring of TATs is occurring along with the investigation of outliers.

The ABG process continues to be refined and team members troubleshoot with the operational staff as needed. Communication between the three departments involved in the process has improved greatly and most concerns are now addressed simply and effectively with a phone call.

Date of Case Study: June, 1994

1997 Epilogue: By way of update on the ABG project, Debra French and Kathy Hermansen said, "Registered nurses, respiratory therapists or patient care technicians now do all inpatient blood draws and the specimens are transported to the lab via the pneumatic tube system as they're drawn. The Laboratory continues to monitor ABG turnaround times and the average TAT continues to be in the 15 to 16 minute range.

"Overall, the hospital's TQM process of using multi-disciplinary teams to address problems is progressing nicely. We have about twice as many teams now, throughout the hospital, and we're seeing some very significant improvements.

"This is very beneficial to the hospital, because it's freeing-up managers to work on new product lines or projects. We're using teams to solve problems with a more structured process, and we believe we're seeing better outcomes as a result."

18

Action Forums Save Big Money, Speed Change at PG&E

SOME RESULTS - 6/93 to 12/96

93 Action Forums (50 to 70 people each)
18% of PG&E employees involved in action forums
   (nearly 50% when mini-forums are counted)
$300 million total savings
$124.50 return for every $1 invested
Documented improvements in:
- Cycle time reduction
- Productivity and performance
- Cost avoidance
- Cost reduction
- Revenue enhancement
- Customer service

OTHER BENEFITS

Managers have a useful change management tool
More cross-functional interactions
Teamwork is learned and fostered
Participants are more committed and satisfied
Culture is changing
PG&E received *Personnel Journal's* 1995 Optimas
   Award in the Financial Impact category.

* * * * *

It was February, 1993.

Utilities throughout the United States had been through nearly 20 years of oil embargoes, rate pressures, mergers and acquisitions, and deregulation.

Pacific Gas & Electric, the largest combined (gas and electric) investor-owned utility in the U.S., with $10 billion in sales, was being buffeted by the most severe competitive and economic storms in its 81-year history. The company needed to freeze utility rates and hiring, to completely reorganize, to significantly cut budgets and layers of management, and to downsize from 24,500 to 20,000 employees.

Yet, it had to continue serving its 9 million customers who inhabit 94,000 square miles of northern and central California.

PG&E's top management realized that if the company continued to do things the way it always had, poor service and declining revenues would follow. Quite the opposite was needed. The question became: how can we simultaneously build superior service and shareholder value—with fewer people?

They concluded that operating managers needed a "change management" tool that would electrify employees and provide a steady charge of new ideas that would lead to a bright future.

Interestingly, the value of that tool had become clear during a tragedy that occurred sixteen months earlier.

Out of the Ashes

"On Sunday, October 20, 1991, 28 people were killed, 3,500 homes were destroyed and more than $6 billion in property was damaged in the Oakland hills fire storm," said Jim Eaneman, a longtime PG&E operations manager who is now manager of human resources development. "Five days later, the gas was running and the lights were on.

"Before the fire storm, we had a rigid command-and-control structure; we had manuals and instructions that specified everything; we essentially told employees to park their minds with the car when they came to work, that we [managers] know best; and we told our customers that we know best.

"What happened in the fire storm was that there was no book. Yes, there had been large fires in outlying areas, but never anything like this in an urban area. The question became, how do you mobilize resources to provide heroic, truly world-class responses to this unprecedented situation?

"The usual response in American business," continued Eaneman, "is to articulate solutions before the problem is fully understood, then throw resources at it. Instead—because there was no book—we found that we had to do things very differently.

"We had a loose structure and incredible cross-communications. We had small teams that went out and assessed the gas and electric situations. We had one person in charge of gas and one in charge of electric and the teams reported to them. We inverted the company pyramid so that the management was supporting the people who were doing the work. We told them, 'This isn't a normal situation. You're the experts. What would you do?'

"And we put a premium on people coming up with new ways to do things—again, because there was no book. New, efficient, economical ways that got the power back on and repairs under way. And they did it!

"For example, there was the matter of all the burned equipment—the poles, the conductors, etc. Normally, a salvage group would take weeks to do estimates. The day after the fire, we had cross-functional teams of materials people and electric operating specialists cataloging the damage using infra-red technology that wasn't prevalent in the corporation at the time. It took them ten hours to get the estimate.

"Working cross-functionally, we never had problems getting supplies and equipment, which was always a bane. And we didn't have one industrial injury...zero!

"A month after the fire storm we surveyed the employees who worked on it and found that it was the highest level of satisfaction ever. They knew their jobs, they knew how they impacted the customer, they felt they were involved, and their effort had been celebrated, recognized, rewarded and reinforced.

"We also surveyed our customers and had almost 100 percent satisfaction...incredible!

"After hearing all this, senior management said to Human Resources, 'Go find us a tool that we can use to replicate what we've learned.' So we searched and found Ord Elliott who had worked with General Electric and had developed an adaptation of GE's Work Out process. We were looking for a change tool that empowered people to actually solve problems, one that we could manage and use without becoming dependent on a consultant long term.

"Importantly, we decided to position the tool as owned by the users, not as an HR binder. And we persuaded senior management that for the first year or two there wouldn't be any targets. We wanted a distributed, iterative evolution rather than a centrally-driven revolution that didn't take.

"They said it best in Collins' and Porras' book, *Built to Last*: 'What we're attempting to do with this is build a clock, not tell the time.'

"We know that there is no panacea or overall prescriptive solution, that not everyone is going to believe in this, and that this is hard work. But it's involved almost half of the employees of the corporation, it's saved or avoided over $300 million in costs, and it has a cost-benefit ratio of $124.50 saved for every dollar we spent. To me, that's a pretty good investment.

"But it goes way beyond that," concluded Eaneman. "People get caught up in this. It gives them power to get things done. It's important to them because they know it lights and heats up people's lives better, both inside and outside the company. Personally, this has been the most rewarding thing I've been associated with in the 28-1/2 years I've been with this corporation."

The Tool and Its Power

"I was one of several hundred consultants that GE used to

implement its Work Out process," said Ord Elliott, president of Implementation Partners. "Here at PG&E we developed a variation of Work Out that better fits this situation and has a more robust front end—in terms of getting people involved, and in developing sponsorship and business commitment for it.

"We decided to take on more than the low-hanging fruit: meatier business problems and a much broader array of issues, such as cycle time reduction in power plants, standardizing electric construction, safety issues and planning processes. We wanted to blast those out and get things done in a very quick period of time.

"We also decided to have a more robust back end—the stage that we call 'accountability manager.' We wanted to make sure that there would be follow-up, that action plans would actually be implemented.

"The beauty of the whole thing is that it's just good management. But that's often not what people do naturally in many companies. In big companies like this, there's a tendency to do a lot of analysis. After you've finished one study, you're not sure, so you need to do another one. By that time, the solutions don't get implemented.

"A crucial element of Action Forums is the decision-making that goes on in the framework phase. In most companies, when groups meet to address a problem, there's too little attention paid to exactly what the problem is, what's needed to solve it, what success would look like, and how that will be measured. Deciding all that leads to knowing who should be there. If you don't have it properly scoped and don't have the right people, a lot of blocks develop down the road. That's why the leadership team is involved in the framework stage. And when it's time to say go or no-go in the Action Forum, the leadership team, augmented by other decision makers, makes a commitment to what's going to get done, by when, and who'll be responsible.

"When those things aren't done in the typical American problem-solving session, nothing comes out of the meeting, decisions aren't made, people get disappointed and disaffected, and a lot of frustration and conflict can come out of it.

"The point is, if you use a discipline to consciously go through the right steps and do the right things, you're going to solve the problem—as long as it's an important, real business problem that's sensible, and a size that you can bite off.

"The problems are usually identified by interviewing managers to learn what business issues are on their plates, and by conducting focus groups with employees in the business units to find out what the people who are doing the work think. You know you have a likely candidate when the management and employee concerns overlap, and they agree that solving it will make the business better and their work lives easier.

"For example, electric construction procedure was identified as being a problem. As a result of the interviews and focus groups, we learned that there were four areas that needed to be focused on and simplified: overhead framing, underground construction, overhead switches and transformers. If those more specific areas could be addressed, there would be big cost savings, more reliability, simpler maintenance and training, and greater safety.

"The idea is not to do everything; the idea is to do something of value so you can get it done, rather than flounder forever. So after 2-1/2 days, the cross-functional teams present their solutions and specific plans directly to the decision-making team, which says yes or no to each of the 50 to 100 recommendations and action items.

"In phase three, 'accountability manager,' there's a 30-, 60- and 90-day follow-up. In fact, the teams have to meet within the first week to get their actions going. In the case of the electric construction procedure follow-up, the four teams came up with some better ideas during the 90 days and got $9 million in cost savings, instead of the $6 million that was estimated.

"It's important to know that the participants are formed into teams at the start of the action forum and stay together through problem-solving, action planning and implementation. The teams identify what they're going to do and are empowered to actually make it happen. Each team has a champion who helps deal with roadblocks and issues and provides a linkage to the decision-making team."

Asked how PG&E dealt with initial resistance to the idea and introduction of Action Forums, Elliott responded, "It was made available and not made mandatory. It was corporately funded, so the business units didn't have to pay for it. Managers were given consultants to learn how to do it, so they could do it on their own. Also, we don't do layoffs as a result of Action Forums; and because of the agreement with the union, there's no job redesign or organizational restructuring. And, it helped for managers to know that the outside consultants were going to disappear, and the company would be self-sufficient.

"Over time, when managers learn the process, the process disappears and they manage differently," concluded Elliott. "It's increased the capability of managers in PG&E to manage change because they've learned how to do it."

From Scared to Confident

"Our group, which is responsible for engineering, construction and maintenance of the transmission system, held the second Action Forum in the company," said Luther Dow, manager of grid maintenance and construction. "I've personally been involved in ten of them.

"That first Action Forum was actually quite scary, because the leadership team had to say 'yes' or 'no', on the spot, to the recommendations. The topics focused on organizational matters. The one that made me most nervous was: Everything you have delegated to you about approving jobs should be delegated. If I said no, they'd say, 'Well, there you go; that shows you how well this process works!'

"Sixty folks were sitting there waiting, wondering whether the leadership team could make a decision—whether or not they were willing to support what seemed to be a reasonable suggestion. Recommendations from the Action Forums are almost always things that are not easy to implement.

"So I said yes, provided there are controls in place. The idea was to decrease the time so job processing could be faster. As it turned out, it's working fine. I've not found any problem with it, whatsoever.

"By our second Action Forum, the union was on board and it was more nuts and bolts—how do we minimize oil leaks and how do we maximize the use of our tree trimming dollars. That one went well, also.

"But the big Action Forums are quite time consuming with 60 people involved for three days. You need those classic Action Forums in the beginning, to have impact and to learn how to do it. However, we realized we needed to integrate them into the workplace. So we trained some second level supervisors to facilitate them and started using mini-Action Forums at the local level. We found that as long as we follow the Action Forum principles—that is, clearly define the problem, get the knowledgeable people and decision makers in the room, make immediate yes/no decisions, and have the people who make the recommendations actually implement them—the process works well for us. I'm really pleased with the way it's working."

Asked whether the process has affected how he thinks and manages, Dow responded: "It's given me a lot more confidence in the department, because employees are coming up with great ideas and following through. I'm becoming much more dependent on them and their knowledge and their inputs. And there are fewer top-down decisions, and more involved decision-making, which is good for the company.

"We're changing from a slow-moving utility to a fast-moving organization. This is an exciting process, it's yielding results, it's changing the way we view decision-making, and it's given us top quality products. You can't ask for much more.

"We have a lot yet to do, but we're a long way from where we were in 1993."

Impact, Impact, Impact

"One of the reasons Action Forums have had a big impact is that they deal with issues that are 'in the face' of managers and employees," said Jim Eaneman. "They're problems that get in their way and that they care about.

"In fact, it's not unusual to hear line people use the word 'passion' in connection with Action Forums. One criterion for selection of topics, issues or problems is whether the employees are passionate about them. And passion is important all the way through implementation.

"Another reason for their impact is that Action Forums are so tightly focused. The problem statement isn't 'Improve customer service;' it's 'How can we get our quality service evaluation up 10 points in installations?' The workforce becomes electrified by such a question and its solution.

"And Action Forums have an impact because knowledgeable people are working on processes, across functions, to make the business work better. That's where a lot of the breakdowns, disconnects and communication problems occur in most businesses: between functions.

"But the thing that causes the most impact—because it puts the teeth in the process—is the accountability manager phase. The power of it is in the follow-through. Just saying you're going to meet again in 30, 60 and 90 days gives you deadlines to work against so you can get results back to the leadership team. It keeps the passion and enthusiasm alive.

"And we can't forget the importance of those big dollar cost savings. The promise of that was critical for top management's initial buy-in. They saw that this wasn't a touchy-feely project, that it was essential for running the business.

"Action forums are a great way of fusing top management's interest in bottom line impact with the workforce's need to have an impact on daily performance."

* * * * *

ACTION FORUM PLAYERS

Leadership Team - Decision makers who scope out the Action Forum, say "yes" or "no" and provide needed support

Action Teams - Cross-functional groups of experts in the topic/issue/problem who are empowered to figure out what to do, get approval and make it happen

Team Champions - Key people, sometimes managers, who obtain information and support for the action teams, and help drive implementation

Facilitators - Experts in the process who make sure the teams are successful

THE PROCESS

1. Framework (2 to 8 weeks)
   - Identify the cross-functional leadership team
   - Specify the topic/issue/problem to be addressed, the boundaries, the desirable results, the success measures, and the required support
   - Identify the champion, facilitators and action team participants
   - Gather data and information that will be needed by the action teams; benchmark other organizations
   - Prepare the logistics, communications and tracking
2. Action Forum (2-1/2 to 3 days)
   - Action teams analyze the topic/issue/problem
   - Identify and prioritize alternative solutions
   - Develop action plan, including steps, target dates and responsible persons
   - Report-out to the leadership team
   - Leadership team approve/disapprove the plan on the spot
3. Accountability Manager (90 days)
   - Action teams implement the action plan with rigorous follow-through

- Leadership team provides needed resources, removes road blocks
- Action teams have 30-, 60- and 90-day status meetings with the leadership team
- Champion and action teams present the final report and celebrate
- Story and outcomes are shared with the broader organization

KEYS TO SUCCESS

- Focus on important, tightly focused business problems that can be solved in 3 months
- Collaboration between decision-makers and employee experts
- Immediate approval of action plan and guarantee of implementation
- Union participation
- Not mandatory
- No job or budget cuts due to action forums

Date of Case Study: January, 1997

19

Chrysler's Continuous Improvement Workshop Process

WORKSHOP RESULTS

Example #1: Sterling Heights Assembly Plant, ABS Subassembly

Walk time reduced from 11 to 1.3 miles per day (88% improvement)

Lead time reduced from 99 to 13 minutes (87% improvement)

Work-in-process reduced from 356 to 59 pieces (83% improvement)

Square foot utilization reduced from 2,014 to 1,200 (40% improvement)

Example #2: Windsor Assembly Plant, Leaf Spring Prep

Productivity increased (pieces/person/shift)—before, 216; after, 360 (67% improvement)

Work-in-process reduced from 84 to 20 pieces (76% improvement)

Floor space 2,389 to 2,229 square feet (7% improvement)

Part travel reduced from 134 to 15 feet (89% improvement)

Walk distance reduced from 64 to 30 feet (53% improvement)

Lead time reduced 32 to 7.5 minutes (76% improvement)

* * * * *

"Of all the quality and productivity improvement tools that we've used since the early 80's, this one is the most effective," said Tom Johnston, general manager, Chrysler Operating System—Manufacturing. "And that includes quality circles, our quality assurance program for suppliers, SPC as a separate initiative, the Crosby quality improvement process, and a lot of productivity initiatives, including efforts to remove redundancies.

"During the last two years we've done more than 500 workshops and we'll do about 700 this year. In cooperation with the UAW locals, we've conducted them in most Chrysler plants and gotten some tremendous results—because the workshops focus on areas needing improvement, and because after one day of training and two days of analysis, the teams just do it."

In addition to talking about the Continuous Improvement Workshop Process, Johnston touched on the company's new overarching Chrysler Operating System (COS), on the educational process related to the new operating system, and on a related implementation innovation called "learning lines." Ben Roush, continuous improvement coordinator at Chrysler's Warren [Michigan] Stamping Plant, and two facilitator colleagues provided a case example of the Continuous Improvement Workshop Process.

How the Workshops Came About

Johnston commented that Chrysler has come back from the precipice of extinction in the early 80's to be solidly competitive again. "Our five platform teams—small cars, large cars, Jeep, truck, and mini-van—our innovative designs that people really love, and our improvement initiatives, have brought us 7 to 10 percent gains in quality every year. We know we can do even better, of course; all of the automotive manufacturers are fighting that battle.

"But in the early '90s, we ran out of cherries to pick and needed to go beyond problem-solving. After Bob Eaton came to Chrysler in 1992 [as Chairman of the Board and Chief Executive Officer], we benchmarked some of the best companies in the U.S. and abroad that have gone through some major cultural changes—Motorola, Xerox, Corning, and others.

"Recommendations coming out of that benchmarking led to our 'Port Huron Experience' which involved most of our executives in sessions on core beliefs, values, and enablers. And some of us attended a workshop put on by the Kaizen Institute where we learned about the importance of 'system' in the Toyota Production System.

"Then I sent some key people to a workshop in the fall of 1993 put on by TBM, Time Based Management. We were all impressed with the fact that you can get a lot done in a very short period of time if you focus a team on a specific area needing improvement.

"In December of that year, we sent quite a number of people to Japan to participate in a TBM-sponsored workshop put on by the Shingujitsu consulting firm which developed the concept of making rapid improvements in a short period of time. Right after that, we put together a team of people to internalize the idea for Chrysler.

"Since the idea wasn't yet approved by our UAW partners under PQI [Partnership for Quality Improvement, the joint Chrysler-UAW effort which started in the early 80's and is at work in 50 locations], we went through a period where we trained some facilitators and had them follow the TBM and Shingujitsu consultants around to observe the process at a number of supplier sites.

"Ultimately, three pilot locations—Warren Stamping, Detroit Axle and Kokomo Transmission—were approved and we started running workshops."

How They Work

Johnston went on to describe the Continuous Improvement Workshop Process, which has a standard 5-day format but has outcomes that are unique in each case. "That's because each workshop is separately planned and focuses on different operations that need different improvements," explained Johnston. "There's a lot of work to planning and running the workshops. Planning is especially important—working on team selection, team leader selection, picking the right area. And sometimes, if the area isn't stabilized, we'll need to do a workshop on quality, productivity, material flow or downtime, first.

"Generally, we pick a subassembly process, part of an assembly line, a machining operation, or a similar area, and set some lofty goals, like 50-80% improvement in work-in-process, lead time, or square-foot utilization.

"From nine to ten people attend each workshop. One-third are usually production associates, one-third come from support areas such as skilled trades, tool engineering and industrial engineering, and one-third are what we call 'new eyes.' They're people who have no familiarization with the area being analyzed, people from anywhere in the corporation who aren't caught up in the area's paradigm and can ask, 'Why do you do this?' Most of Chrysler's executives have attended workshops as 'new eyes.'

"The first day consists of six to eight hours of training on concepts such as the Toyota Production System, waste and what it is, Just-In-Time, standardization, levelled and balanced schedules, the 5 S's, standard operating procedures, etc.

"The second day, the group gathers information, collects data and analyzes it.

"On the third day, they get into the Do phase. And this is important. All of our workshops are 'learn and do.' We want them to move equipment, if that's appropriate, to define standard operating procedures, to establish the 5S's. Moving equipment right away is a big thing; normally it takes six months to move anything.

"The fourth day is for making additional adjustments and improvements, and on the fifth day they do a presentation to plant management, local union leadership, engineering, and production area managers, and there's a celebration of the team's success.

"They're also to develop a 30-day list—things that couldn't be completed during the workshop that should be finished right away. When it's all done, we want the results—and we're getting impressive results—but we also want people to feel good that their area is clean and comfortable, and we want to know that appropriate ergonomic improvements have been made.

"On the flip side, we have to be careful about how things are done. Moving equipment is like someone moving furniture in your house; without your input and consent there would be a problem. And people have concerns about their jobs."

Johnston went on to explain that the Continuous Improvement Workshop Process isn't used only to improve current operations; some workshops focus on the future. "We do a lot of pre-production workshops," he said. "And these probably have the greatest leverage for us, because if we can get the production process properly established before we put the equipment in, we won't repeat some earlier mistakes and we'll be able to optimize the efficiencies before we get into production. Warren Stamping's workshops this week are an example."

An Example: Warren Stamping

"We were one of the pilot sites chosen 2-1/2 years ago to conduct the workshops under the UAW-Chrysler PQI umbrella," said Ben Roush, continuous improvement coordinator for the Warren Stamping Plant. "We co-determined it with our union local, and have complete support from both sides on doing this.

"Our plant controller verified that the workshops saved $4 million in 1994, $3 million in 1995, and we expect double that in 1996 when we've got 80 events scheduled. The controller won't count an improvement unless it's been sustained for at least six weeks. We've found that if you support the workers, they'll keep tweaking the improvement and it will be sustained.

"A lot of these workshops come from our plant's goals and objectives—improve quality, cost and delivery. For example, reduce the downtime on a particular line so our productivity numbers come up. So we get a workshop together and focus on downtime on that line.

"The four teams we've got going this week are numbers 51, 52, 53 and 54. They're pre-production workshops; the teams are doing actual line design for our factory's stamping of the major panel assemblies for the 1999 Jeep Grand Cherokee. Some of our outside engineers came to us with concepts and we're shrinking them down, pacing them with our customer's demand rate and leaning the lines down.

"There's a team working on the front doors, one on the rear doors, one is doing the lift gate, and the fourth is doing the hood. We did this two years ago and those lines are now being implemented and will launch in July.

"These teams are early in the fourth day of the workshop and have developed prototype panels and composites; they've gone through a lot of the layout, value added, non-value added and all the processing of the stations. They've come up with a design that's U-shaped instead of a long line, which will bring the operators together in one island of work. This is a pretty intensive week, with many long days. It's not an 8-to-5 educational experience; we're very serious about this.

"The teams have objectives for the week that have to do with quality, productivity, capital cost, square-foot utilization, lead time and take time [pace]. Instead of running the line at our usual 20 seconds on one shift, we're looking to run it at our customer's demand rate: 32 seconds over two shifts. That should help us with overproduction, downtime, quality problems and extra inventory. And we won't need extra tooling, which should help reduce vendor costs."

Providing more background on the workshops at Warren Stamping, Roush said: "PQI is the umbrella for both the PQI teams and the Continuous Improvement Workshop process. Our PQI teams are the heart and soul of the workshop process, because the players for the workshops come from the PQI teams.

"PQI teams are improvement teams that meet regularly to work on quality and productivity. We record their activities on a large board in the PQI meeting room to make sure they're active. You've got to have the people on the floor actively involved in making improvements or you're bound to fail.

"We've got 89 active PQI teams, more than any other Chrysler facility. Fifty-six percent of our plant's 3,000 people are on PQI teams: skilled trades and production people; managers and supervisors also. In fact, participation is in their objectives.

"The PQI teams and workshops are going well because it's a joint effort with the UAW, and because we have considerable autonomy. Things work better when a plant does it themselves."

Harvey Whitehead and Lavonne Summers are PQI facilitators who, respectively, represent management and the UAW. "The workshops are a tool under our partnership that we use to get results," said Whitehead. "People love to be part of results-oriented work. Not only are PQI team members involved in the workshops, they're part of the follow-up after the workshops are finished."

"It's a tool for our use," agreed Summers. "We're good here, because of it. Our plant manager and local union president had the foresight to see that this will work, and that what it takes is people working together."

"And it's important that Ben is inside the building," added Whitehead. "If he was outside the building, he'd just be counting the number of workshops he facilitated. This way, he does the planning with the staff, through the goals and objectives. He's got ownership. And he's part of the follow-up after the workshops.

"Ben, Lavonne, Jerry Durden, the plant COS coordinator, and I are all responsible for checking the follow-through on the 30 day list. And the items get completed 90-95% of the time."

Continued Roush, "The workshops don't always work. But they usually do, and the turning point is when people who have been quiet for two days see that we're actually willing to do something physical, like move equipment. Then they pull out their list of things *they'd* like to see improved. We recently had to move some control panels, at a cost of $40,000. That really showed people we're serious!"

"On the fourth day of a workshop, we once shut down the line for an hour in one production area; that's pretty serious, too, because we're a Just-In-Time plant," said Whitehead. "We did it to make some adjustments on a robot because we weren't hitting our numbers. On the 57th minute, with the production people standing there ready to go back to work, we held our breaths until we saw it work. It was very exciting to see a workshop team come up with a solution and make it work right then and there."

"The workshops are a get-it-done, results-oriented approach," continued Roush. "The best events are those that are planned well and get results during the week. But we don't normally talk about dollar savings at the end of the workshop. We recognize and celebrate the effort. To get the *effort,* you've got to have the environment that allows the teams to *try.* We have the opportunity here to give some things a try. And, consequently, we get good results."

Chrysler Operating System

"The Continuous Improvement Workshop Process is one of the tools in our Chrysler Operating System," said Tom Johnston. "We began defining and developing the operating system in late '93 and it's still evolving to fit our culture. That's what we expect to be teaching soon on the first day of the workshops instead of the Toyota Production System. It'll be more relevant to our people and tie everything together.

"The Chrysler Operating System is clearly the way we want to do business as a manufacturing organization. We've got full-time COS specialists in most of our plants to help make it happen.

"What's really important is to have an overall system and a balance between its subsystems, rather than concluding that the answer is quality circles, or Just-In-Time, or some such solution which is just the tip of the iceberg. The four underlying subsystems, as we define them, are human infrastructure, waste elimination or value-added activities, robust and capable processes, and leveled and balanced schedules. There should be a solid interaction between those subsystems.

"For example, if you go out on a line and find that an operation isn't robust and capable—that there's a quality problem—the reason may be that you haven't trained people, that you're not doing preventive maintenance, or that your schedules are bouncing around too much or you're running ten-hour shifts seven days a week and can't get people in to do PM. Or from the standpoint of value-added activities, you may not be making progress on productivity because you don't have robust and capable processes, because of the human infrastructure, or because you don't have leveled and balanced schedules. So the Chrysler Operating System has become the framework for our thinking and acting on these things.

"For each of these four subsystems we've identified support processes that help us achieve what we need to achieve. For example, under human infrastructure, how we recruit and hire people is an important process. We need to work on all of those processes so the subsystems will work well together.

"And, for each support process, we've defined the tools that are appropriate. We've always had programs of the month. Now, any new tools will have to fit in with what we're trying to achieve. As an example, activity-based costing tells us where we're spending our money, which will help us eliminate waste. Another is QS9000; without the Chrysler Operating System, we would have said QS9000 is something different, but with it we can see how it fits in and supports what we're trying to do overall."

The COS Education Process

"We've developed a series of five classes to educate our manufacturing managers about the Chrysler Operating System," continued Johnston. "Dennis Pawley, our executive vice president of manufacturing has been the first person to teach all five classes to his direct reports, who then teach their direct reports, and finally the plant managers teach their staffs. We believe that the bosses need to learn these things and that this is a good way for that to happen.

"These one-day classes have been set up primarily not to develop skills, but to develop an understanding of gaps in the way we do business and to begin highlighting things that we need to work on. In fact, consistent with our 'learn and do' philosophy, there was an assignment after each class for people to do and to report back on at the next class.

"The first class compared the way we do business with the best in the world, to show the gaps. We used a couple of case studies from Harvard as well as one from our plants. The second class was about robust and capable processes.

"In the third class, we went back to basics and challenged people to find out whether they were really doing standardized work, whether SPC is being used effectively, whether preventive maintenance is really being done, whether they've done anything with the 5S's. We found that we weren't doing as well as we should—as compared with the best in the world.

"The next class taught waste elimination and measurement, which included an exercise of walking a production line looking for various kinds of waste and convinced people they could do better.

"The fifth class dealt with the subject that's probably most important in all of this, which is human infrastructure—especially the role of the leader. Over the years, we've found that it's really difficult to hold the improvements after workshops, and that one of the biggest reasons is that the leadership on the plant floor doesn't follow through."

Learning Lines

"As part of the Chrysler Operating System education process, we've chosen an area of every plant that we call the 'learning line' to work on," continued Johnston. "As we teach the concepts, we're trying to do them in real work environments. We want people to really dig in and find out what's going on and what needs to happen.

"For instance, on standard operating procedures, are we really involving the operators; are we getting consensus on the best way to do the job; are we developing instructions that are clear and visible? Without standard operating procedures, people are doing things differently shift-to-shift or when someone is absent. Also, if you don't actually do preventive maintenance, you'll pay for it later. And if you don't focus on the 5 S's, you don't know how important it is to have a place for everything and everything in its place.

"A thing as simple as finding a broom out of place ought to tell you there's something wrong. Somebody must have been sweeping up something; what were they sweeping up and why were they sweeping it up?

"Learning lines have provided the practical application of the Chrysler Operating System education, and they've been helpful to the plants as well.

"Learning in general is something we're getting better at in Chrysler. We've been in trouble a number of times, so we're more open to change. It's caused us to do some things, like these workshops and the Chrysler Operating System, that are really going to help us in the long run."

Date of Case Study: March, 1996

1997 Epilogue: "Ten months later, things are still proceeding as reported in the case study," said Tom Johnston. "The workshops, training, PQI, learning lines and Chrysler Operating System continue to be very important to our improvement efforts and our future.

"To us, empowering people to improve operations and help with pre-production planning is the way to go."

20

Managing Through Teams at AT&T Microelectronics

PROFILE

Organization: AT&T Microelectronics Orlando, plant, a complementary metal oxide semiconductor wafer fabrication facility.
Products: Integrated circuits for a wide array of OEM devices such as computer peripherals, drive controllers, network switching machines, and advanced business and cellular telecommunications products.
Customers: AT&T, Seagate, Western Digital, Adaptec, Apple, Sun Microsystems, Zenith, and others.
Employees: About 800.
Location: Orlando, Fla.
Award: Winner of the 1994 Shingo Prize for Excellence in Manufacturing. [The prize is named for Shigeo Shingo, a key developer of Just-In-Time manufacturing, and is administered by Utah State University.]

* * * * *

"We've got the traditional organizational chart, with the usual kinds of key managers doing the usual things," said Pat Lane, quality manager at AT&T Microelectronics' plant in Orlando, Florida.

"But if you manage only in the traditional way, a lot of things fall between the cracks. We found that we needed to set up another structure—with several kinds of teams—to manage our cross-functional activities, to achieve goals and objectives, and to improve aspects of quality that wouldn't be addressed in a traditional environment."

A Revolutionary Approach

"We began creating our team structure in 1985," Lane continued. "Our plant director, then the late Bob Visco, had declared from the start that we were going to have participative management. We all looked at him and wondered, 'What in the world is that?'

"A year earlier, people from all over the country had been drawn to Orlando to start this new plant. Visco vowed that Orlando would be different. He hired the Rensis Likert consulting firm to help us, and at first the experience was frustrating. We wanted them to tell us what to do. Instead, they worked with us to get *us* to say what was right for us.

"We developed a team focus from the beginning. Our core belief was that although people individually can do a good job, by combining their forces the ultimate product would be better than any one person could achieve alone."

Informal Teams

"Over the years, we developed a way of teaming that is both formal and informal," explained Lane. "An example of our informal teams are what we call natural work groups. These are people who work together because they need each other to do their job. Each natural work group really is a team and works pretty much on its own.

"A good example is process engineering, which has more than 40 engineers reporting to one manager. The manager has no intermediate levels. But just from an administrative standpoint, one manager can't deal with that large a group. So each processing area is a team with a technical leader, not a supervisor. The manager depends on these teams to run their jobs. The teams work together, and their leaders deal with cross-topic areas.

"This arrangement came about as a natural evolution of the way we work. No one told us to do this. It's just the way we do our jobs. One consultant who was visiting us said, 'You folks are a riot. Based on your organizational chart, you have the most hierarchal, strict structure we've ever seen. But you don't work anything like that. You have teams and your teams work with other teams, and everybody's interacting with each other. Some people don't even know who their bosses are!'"

Formal Teams Developed Through Trial and Error

Continued Lane, "Besides the natural work groups, we have a formal team system that came about by trial and error. No one from management said, 'Let's have a team.' Instead, back in 1984, people said, 'Let's get together off the floor and work on this problem for a half hour. I bet we could come up with something better.' So in different areas teams sprung up that we called grass roots teams because they had no sponsor. The problem was, there was no common methodology.

"When the consulting group came, they helped us set up several formalized teams. These handled issues that weren't anyone's job — the soft-side, human issues that didn't fall under quality, engineering or other functions. One of these was the A-Team, which still exists today. It's made up of union and management representatives from several organizations in the plant.

"The A-Team evolved over the years, partly because we later developed a more formal structure of cross-functional teams to cover some of those gaps. The A-Team still raises issues that concern people, but it has become primarily an information dissemination tool. It's sort of a traffic cop who sees that issues are brought to the appropriate group."

Management Involvement was Requested

"When the grass roots teams began asking for help in solving problems, a group calling themselves the Support Group came together to support them," said Lane. "The Support Group said a standardized methodology for solving problems was needed. Part of me said, 'Don't mess with a good thing.' On the other hand, I agreed some standardization would be good because, as it was, everyone was speaking a different language.

"So, the Support Group developed a training program that worked well for a few years. Then one day they said to management, 'We think you need to get involved in what's going on. We need more structure to this process.'

"The Support Group was afraid that teams were working on things that weren't aligned with the corporation's goals. They also wanted to avoid duplicating efforts and wasting resources. But they didn't feel they were the ones to question managers about projects.

"What resulted was that management appointed a team coordinator. Eventually the Support Team became the Coordination Team, with the coordinator as team leader. As the number of teams grew, however, the Coordination Team told management a Steering Group was needed.

"The team brought in a speaker from another AT&T location to spend a Saturday in an all-day session for management in training and team building. From that, management determined what their role would be as a Steering Committee.

"As time went on, however, we became increasingly concerned about the lack of continuity between our quality system and what teams were doing. The Steering Committee reviewed teams very well, but wasn't tying the teams into the plant's quality system. Most of the teams were doing projects that supported the business, but we couldn't document this. We proposed that management form a Quality Council.

"We also created process management teams, called Lead Teams, to own the space between the functional organizations. You won't find functional managers in charge of these spaces. They're the cracks that things kept falling into. These teams fill the gaps."

Types of Quality Teams

Team	Mission	Members	Meets	Examples
Lead Team	Oversight Guidance Support Implementation Process mgmt. Select areas for improvement	Appointed by managers (may also be volunteers with manager buy-in) Minimum of one manager per Lead Team	As needed, at least monthly	Recognition Coordination TRAPT SPC
Improvement Teams (QI's)	Identify, analyze and solve problems Teams are ongoing and use a standard methology		Weekly	
• Voluntary	Teams select their own issues to work on	Volunteers from a single work area (functional) or multiple work groups (cross functional)		MOS Teams, i.e. Chip-N-Dip Penny-Pinchers SPC Teams
• Appointed	Teams are given their improvement area/topic	Team members are assigned by managers and/or Lead Team		
Task Teams	Analyze and solve assigned problems Teams disband when problem is solved	Appointed by managers; either functional or cross-functional	As needed	Design Team, Process Change Team

Teams Are Pervasive

Today, nearly half of AT&T Orlando's workforce is involved on structured teams, which are primarily quality improvement (QI) teams [see box]. Directly supporting QI teams are the Lead Teams, and supporting them is the Quality Council made up of top management and representatives from the union and from each Lead Team.

Four of the Lead Teams—Statistical Process Control, Make Orlando Successful (MOS), Orlando Affirmative Action Committee (ORAAC), and Information Technologies—each oversees up to 10 or more QI teams. The remaining four Lead Teams each oversees a specific area: training, recognition, engineering, or ISO 9002. In addition, there are the natural work teams and numerous task teams, which come and go as managers see a need to solve a particular problem or address an issue.

Over the entire team structure is the top management team,

headed by Plant Director Bob Koch, who followed Visco in 1990.

"Our underlying philosophy is that you need to have as much broad participation as possible," said Koch. "Consensus is more than just a wonderful notion of how to solve problems. With broad involvement, broad participation, and consensus on decisions, employees can move ahead and implement programs.

"One of the things we've been trying to do with teams is take a lot of the decisions out of the hierarchical structure. AT&T used to be about as hierarchal as you could imagine. There were layers and levels and all the decisions bubbled up and came back down. That's not the best way to run a business. The people closest to the details make the best decisions. So we've been consciously pushing team decision-making. And we've done it as much to drive quality improvement as to change our management style.

"Not only are we driving ownership down through the organization," said Koch, "we're spreading more ownership across the staff. A few years ago, we had loosely-knit functional managers who took ownership only of their own areas.

"During the past few years, I've emphasized that we're a board of directors. As a staff, we own the company and we have to get out of our individual boxes and start looking at the overall management of the facility. After a few sessions with consultants, our managers started to function much more like a team."

Empowerment Includes Upward Delegation

"One of the things I've learned about empowering people is that their biggest fear is they'll fail the boss who empowered them," reflected Koch. "For example, when we had our first ISO 9002 audit, instead of being concerned about passing the audit, our ISO Team was more concerned that I'd be upset if we didn't pass. I never doubted. I knew we would score high.

"We always think about empowering people as being one-directional—down. Our people have taught me that empowerment also goes the other way. They're very good at upward delegation. Once they've been entrusted with things to do, if they run into roadblocks, they come to me and say, 'You've got to clear this roadblock, or barrier, or problem.' My job is to do what the employees ask me to do to make their job easier. So, empowerment works both ways.

"The other side of empowerment is that managers need to say, 'I don't know. I don't have the answers. I know where we need to get to. I'm not sure about the how. You've got to help me know how to get there.' People get a lot more charged up when they realize the boss is letting them know they know as much as he or she does. This has been a struggle, but we're getting better.

"For example, when we started our training team, which is a cross-section of people, they said, 'What's our job?' I said, 'It's to put together a training program to improve the performance of every employee in the factory.' They left, then came back a few minutes later and said, 'Tell us again. Someone up there has always told us what employees are to be trained in. What do you want?'

"I said, 'I'm not smart enough to tell you what you need.' So now they've done surveys and canvassed people to find out what's needed. They're basing the training on the associates' needs, not on what management thinks they need.

"This kind of thing is starting to happen all over the organization as more and more managers drive down ownership of the daily activities. The people are rather surprised because we've had a culture of being told what to do and now we're trying to come up with a culture that engages the person's brain and gets him or her more involved. And it's beginning to work. Our teams are paying off."

Teams Bring Impressive Achievements

Just some of the results from Orlando's team approach include:
- 20% + reduction in defect density every six months since 1991
- 45% reduction in wafer scrap since 1991
- 46% reduction in rework since 1991
- Received ISO 9002 registration in 1993

- Received OSHA's highest award for Safety and Environment Protection, Star Status in the Voluntary Protection Program
- Winner of the 1994 Shingo Prize for Excellence in Manufacturing.

One team alone, the Chip and Dip Team, identified and solved a problem in manufacturing integrated circuits, and is saving AT&T Orlando $2.45 million annually because of it.

"The team was formed in 1990 and has worked on yearly projects ever since, as well has having a lot of quick successes in-between," said JoAnn Newman, information technologies manager. "One of our most significant accomplishments was our recent particle production project that focused on the rinsers/dryers in the chemical area. The equipment tended to generate a lot of particles, which are very detrimental to the product.

"To find the root cause, we followed the QI story methodology and let the data point us in the right direction. Someone suspected a new piece of equipment, but the data clearly showed that rinsers/dryers were what we should be working on. There were two main issues: the filters and the nitrogen pressure."

Explained Steve Gunter, chemical process engineer, "Preventive Maintenance had a laundry list of what they were to do and when it was done, they would say, 'PM complete.' But they didn't say what they did specifically, such as changing filters or greasing bearings. We found a pretty serious discrepancy in withdrawals of filters from the storeroom. When PM should have withdrawn 50, only 10 were withdrawn. So we changed all the filters and updated the PM procedures, making filter changes a separate entity."

"The second major root cause was nitrogen pressure," said Newman. "If pressure is too high, it increases particulates. The gauges aren't easy to get to and the pressure wasn't being routinely checked. When we checked them, they were inaccurate. Now we've implemented a regular maintenance check. By finding these two root causes, we're getting three more chips per wafer, which doesn't sound like much, but it adds up to a significant dollar payback."

Said Pat Connor, reports and results specialist, "We feel good about the project because so much work was behind it and everyone took part. We actually saw that the process works. All of this has increased our respect for each other and taught us to value everybody's talents."

Added Gunter, "In the past, we had a specific team leader for each major project. Now we've adopted a new teamwork concept and are taking turns in roles. For a month, someone is team leader, someone else takes minutes or is scrap supervisor. So instead of having one person in charge, ours is a team effort."

Teams Focus on Plant Goals

"More and more, everything here is done with a quality process," said Plant Director Koch. "We've attempted to move under our Quality Council everything that people impact or that impacts people.

"We've got a lot of team activity going on. And, at the same time, we have goals and objectives from the corporation, from which we develop our plant goals and objectives. We make sure everyone —engineers, supervisors, and quality teams—also develop goals and objectives consistent with those of the plant.

"As we began our quality process, it became obvious that we also needed mission and vision statements to see long-term where we're going. At times when we're in a staff meeting, we have to hold up these statements and say, 'Does what we're discussing have anything to do with our mission and vision? If it doesn't, disregard it.'

"Because I'm a believer in relationship before task, we've spent a lot of time building relationships," continued Koch. "We've found that if these work effectively, we can solve any problem.

"We're moving away from things that in the past were counter to teamwork, such as individual recognition programs. These tend to destroy teamwork. Now we have a Recognition Team managing our recognition. When we recently passed ISO 9002, the Recognition Team had an ISO celebration party. At other times, they'll have a

MOS Teams recognition party, a sharing rally, or other event.

"And relationships shouldn't be destroyed arbitrarily either. For example, we've developed an economic model and it shows that layoffs are counterproductive in our business. Unless you can see for certain a downturn lasting for at least 18 months, there's no cost benefit to laying off people. With layoffs, you have a 10 percent loss in yield for three months. Then, when you hire workers back months later, you have another hidden five percent loss. And, while you're adjusting both of those times, you're increasing overtime by 10 percent."

Looking at Self-directed Teams

"We've taken participative management about two-thirds down in the organization," said Koch. "We're about to get to the last third, which is engaging our hourly people more in the ownership of the business and managing it day to day."

Added Tom Christian, president of Local 2000 of the International Brotherhood of Electrical Workers, "I've been very pleased that we have a team structure here. You don't have to be involved, but I encourage people to do so. The jury is still out, however, on whether it's right for our culture to move to self-directed teams. My gut feeling is that the type of work we do won't lend itself to a self-directed workforce.

"I've seen facilities where self-directed teams are in place and it's very easy for them to tell who their customers and suppliers are. But in our environment, we have many customers at different levels and stages. Nevertheless, we've got people out visiting other companies to learn as much as we can about them."

"The team structure we have is definitely right for us," concluded Lane. "But they have to be doing the right things for the business. It's got to be both. Teams for their own sake won't work. We find them particularly important in managing the white spaces—to keep those tasks that don't seem to belong to anyone from falling through the cracks."

Date of Case Study: August 1994

1997 Epilogue: Since this case study was written, the Orlando plant became part of Lucent Technologies and has recently become the single semiconductor manufacturing site for a joint venture between Lucent and Cirrus Semiconductor, with Bob Koch reporting to the company's CEO. The new company is called Cirent Semiconductor.

According to Pat Lane, "Our teams have continued to function well under AT&T and Lucent. And they'll definitely continue to function under Cirent. But, all of our activities are currently being re-evaluated, and everything will change to some degree or other. Come back in a year for the sequel!"

Part Five

Self-Directed Teams: The Ultimate in Empowerment— 4 Case Studies

"People wish to produce quality; they wish to have pride in workmanship."
—W. Edwards Deming

21

Empowerment Boundaries at Saturn

At Saturn, ultimate responsibility for effective organization of work resides in work units (self-directed work teams). A work unit is defined as an integrated group of approximately six to fifteen team members. Each work unit has 29 functions. All functions assume knowledge and support of pertinent Saturn production systems, commitment to world-class quality, concern for customer enthusiasm and respect for individual team members. The 29 functions are as follows:

Each Work Unit...

1. **...Applies Consensus Decision-making.** Input and buy-in from all team members of the unit are required for major decisions. Consensus is achieved when everyone (not majority rule) is 70% comfortable with a decision and 100% committed to its implementation. Anyone against a decision must provide a reasonable and timely alternative.
2. **...Is Self-managed.** Work units accomplish their responsibilities (and make operational and planning decisions) without external control, and without permanent internal leaders; leadership shifts among members regularly in the role of the Work Unit Counselor. Individual members are accountable for their own behavior.
3. **...Makes Its Own Job Assignments.** Work units identify job elements, which are then distributed equally among every member of the team and in accordance with needs of

safety, effectiveness and efficiency.

4. **...Resolves Its Own Conflicts.** Problems are approached from a "win-win" or "no deal" perspective. Only after effort to resolve conflicts internally is intervention sought from outside.

5. **...Plans Its Own Work.** Each work unit understands its purpose, understands the Saturn Production System, and analyzes its tasks and responsibilities. The work unit sets priorities to finish the work on time and to the customers' satisfaction.

6. **...Designs Its Own Jobs.** Jobs are designed at the work unit level to achieve tasks and responsibilities. It is up to the work unit to balance people, technical and financial resources, to succeed and to continuously improve.

7. **...Controls Its Own Scrap.** Units control their own scrap, thereby minimizing waste, supporting the budget and often benefiting the environment.

8. **...Controls Its Own Material and Inventory.** Saturn work units deal directly with suppliers, partners, customers and indirect/product material resource team members to successfully fulfill their role within the Saturn Production System.

9. **...Performs Its Own Equipment Maintenance.** To the extent that expertise, ability, knowledge and safety conditions make it possible, a work unit performs its own equipment maintenance.

10. **...Performs Its Own Direct/Indirect Work.** Work units perform their own work based on customer requirements. Each unit identifies its needs while planning for the effective use of people in order to accomplish the necessary tasks in accordance with the Saturn Production System.

11. **...Schedules Its Own Communications Inside and Outside the Group.** A work unit maintains effective and timely means of communication among team members, as well as with others external to the team.

12. **...Keeps Its Own Records.** Each work unit develops and maintains records that will help its members efficiently perform in a cost-effective manner. When needed, the work unit can get assistance in determining what records need to be maintained and will be provided necessary resources to produce and store records.
13. **...Constantly Seeks Improvement in Quality, Cost and the Work Environment.** The work unit involves all members in improving quality, costs, and the work environment.
14. **...Performs To Its Own Budget.** Work units plan their own budgets in concert with Saturn budgetary procedures and the business plan. They track costs and are accountable for their budget performance—one of the measures of continuous improvement.
15. **...Integrates Horizontally With Business Unit Resources.** Work units understand their interdependent roles and responsibilities and are integrated horizontally. Business unit and module resources are available for work unit needs.
16. **...Reflects Synergistic Group Growth.** Work units seek synergy: the process of the whole group producing at a greater rate than the sum of individuals working alone.
17. **...Determines Its Own Methods.** Each work unit is responsible for generating successful work methods consistent with the Saturn Production System. This can range from designating jobs, to comprehending necessary resources (e.g., layout, tools, equipment, ergonomics, etc.) and balancing pursuit of a fixed plan with flexibility for continuous improvement.
18. **...Schedules Its Own Relief.** Work units provide their own relief, scheduled and unscheduled. They strive to balance human needs with work requirements consistent with the Saturn Production System.
19. **...Schedules Its Own Vacations.** Work units plan and coordinate members' vacations without compromise to the needs

of people and the Saturn Production System.

20. **...Provides for Its Own Absentee Replacements.** Each work unit monitors members' attendance. Each also plans for and provides coverage without compromise to quality or the production schedule.

21. **...Performs Its Own Repairs.** In the event a job leaves a work unit with a known or unknown non-conformance to specification, the originating work unit will be accountable for corrective action and repair.

22. **...Performs Its Own Housekeeping.** Work units do their own housekeeping to maintain a safe and clean work area. (Saturn may choose to provide some of the facility's cleaning through external resources.)

23. **...Maintains and Performs Its Own Health and Safety Program.** Each work unit keeps proper and timely records on health and safety information and training for individual members. The work unit ensures that health and safety is of the utmost importance to individual members. Saturn will comply with all federal, state and local regulations and will provide the work unit with the necessary resources to do so.

24. **...Is Responsible for Producing Quality Products on Schedule at Competitive Costs.** Each work unit has responsibility for producing world-class quality products on schedule and at competitive costs. Team members focus on customer satisfaction with emphasis on continuous improvement.

25. **...Assists in Developing and Delivering Its Own Training.** Each work unit identifies the unit's training needs and available resources, plus provides primary delivery of information or skills to unit members.

26. **...Obtains Its Own Supplies.** Each work unit orders its own indirect material requirements from primary suppliers.

27. **...Seeks the Resources It Needs.** Work units identify and seek resources as needed through the module advisors and

business unit.

28. **...Schedules and Holds Its Own Meetings.** Self-directed work units set the frequency and duration of meetings needed to run their part of the business in concert with the Saturn Production System.

29. **...Initiates the Consultative Procedure for Self-corrective Action, with Responsibility on the Individual Member.** The work unit establishes and ensures behavioral norms consistent with Saturn's Mission, Philosophy and shared value system. In doing so, it also implements the consultation process, emphasizing the individual members' responsibility to initiate self-corrective action.

© 1996 Saturn Corporation, Used With Permission.

22

Managing the Change to Self-directed Work Teams at Harris Semiconductor

In 1989, Melbourne, Florida-based Harris Semiconductor began what they called "climbing the mountain of change." But it was one thing to decide that their 9,000-person business needed changing, and quite another to manage change so that it was win-win for everyone—the company, management, and employees.

Harris' Semiconductor Sector manufactures discrete semiconductors and integrated circuits for analog and digital signal processing and power applications.

The sector's goal was to develop an organization that focused on problem-solving, continuous quality improvement, and employee participation in the business. After assessing initiatives already in place, they concluded that transitioning to self-directed work teams (SDWTs) was critical to achieving their objectives.

But, for the most part, the organization had to make this radical change without a guide because, unlike today, there were no models and very few books and resources about SDWTs. Harris soon found that to successfully implement SDWTs, a structure for change was absolutely vital. By trial-and-error, the structure they arrived at included: 1) a four-step management-of-change process; 2) the design of the change process; 3) team developmental stages; 4) training in social, technical, and administrative skills; and 5) team recognition.

Plant Manager Ray Odom, Training Manager Ed Rose, and

Fabrication Technologists Phyllis Davis and Sofia Davis talked about how this structure helped them successfully transition to a new and more rewarding way of doing business.

Our Management Style Needed an Overhaul

"Changing to self-directed work teams five years ago was an attempt to utilize the collective intellect of our entire organization," said Odom. "We wanted to get more than just the people's hands and feet, which is what we were getting. We were telling them what to do, when, and how, and we basically said, 'We do all the thinking. You just do what you're told.'

"In the past, we would have said our most valuable asset was our equipment because we're a relatively capital-intensive industry. Now, we've made a fundamental change in our thinking that recognizes our people are most valuable.

"I love to tell about Ed and me. Before our change process, he had been the traditional production manager who got a lot accomplished by how loud he yelled. I was in engineering and got things done—it didn't matter if I left a wake of bodies in my path. But I didn't feel very good when I went home at night, because I knew what approach I was using.

"Our culture almost encouraged this kind of behavior, but I credit our senior management for recognizing that it wasn't the way we wanted to run the organization. So, we went through a cultural change that occurred not by evolution, but by revolution. We attended cultural meetings off-site to talk about how we were currently running the business and how we would like to run it. We decided we were going to be successful in a different manner.

"I was very happy to get involved and tried to change my style overnight. In Ed's case, we had to take him out of his job to change his style. His initial reaction was, 'All I know how to do is production management.' But I said I'd like him to be the training/facilitator person and find a way to correct the management style of our production managers and supervisors.

"It was one of the better moves in Ed's career because I haven't seen anyone who's gotten into a change in roles as eagerly and actively as he has. It was almost like this new role was his 'calling.' He's very energetic and enthusiastic and relates very well because he can say, 'I can tell you from experience.'"

Four Groups Mapped Our Current and Ideal States

"We brought in a consultant—Larry Miller of Atlanta—who had a process called Quality by Design," continued Odom. " This takes a cross-functional group of people and gives them the responsibility to map the current work-and-information flow, what the ideal state would be, and the variances between the two.

"We chose people from four areas to be our design teams—a front-end operation, wafer fabrication, back-end operations, assembly and test, and a business unit. They received training and were facilitated by our Organizational Development group. The four teams went off for three or four months and, when they returned, gave reports.

"Although each presentation was different, they were similar in that they all recommended we form semi-autonomous work teams. Another of their recommendations was that we break down the organization's symbols. Traditional management had the managers in white shirts and ties and workers in blue collars. Management had parking spaces, workers had general parking. It was a class system that wasn't helping us to be a successful organization. Now, we're a casual workplace and everyone parks in the general area, whether they're the sector president or a production worker."

Began Experimenting With SDWTs in Two Pilot Programs

"Another manager, Steve Titus, and I took champion roles and said we'd begin working with self-directed work groups in our fabrication areas," recalled Odom. "Together, this involved about 400 people out of about 3,000. The organization established a steering team comprised of the plant manager and his staff. And Steve and I presented regular reviews to keep them up-to-date on what we were doing.

"We each took different approaches to implementing self-directed work teams. Mine was more formalized and more structured. We required every team to go through specific activities, and they were strongly facilitated through each. There also was reporting guidance. Steve's approach was more informal and structured differently, but worked well also.

"I learned from this experience that there are different ways to achieve the same ends. The idea is to get the team involved in the business, give them the information they need to make the right decisions, and then get out of their way. You're there as support. This doesn't happen as easily as I've stated, however. It was a tremendous amount of work.

"Up front, we explained that we were trying something new and didn't have models or books to help us, but had received training and recommendations from consultants. We told our people that our goal was to make us better at producing wafers; we warned that we probably would make mistakes along the way and might have to back up and start down another path.

"Whenever we changed direction, we explained why. Often during the process, we'd ask our people what they would do in a situation, and we'd have open discussion. We were running four shifts and would pull all the people into a meeting room to discuss the issue. This went a very long way toward building trust between the management team and workforce.

"We always had a very vocal group which were resistant to the change. As a management team, we listened and tried to convince them that our direction was right. We asked them to go along with us, even if they didn't agree. Eventually, those people became vocal on the positive side; that's when I realized the process was working."

Always Focused on the Reason for the Change

"If you think this is an easier way to manage, you're wrong," said

Odom. "It takes more time and energy because you're dealing not only with the work, but with people and the social activities in the area. In the past, you only had to deal with work flow, and the social issues were handled by supervisors. But if you believe SDWTs are the way to go, you have to get involved in the social issues, as well.

"There's a fine line between self-direction and anarchy. You have to be very careful as you implement this process because you're telling people that you're empowering them. But you've got to keep reminding them what the reason for the change is: so we'll be better at what we're doing. We're not forming SDWTs to put carpet in the break rooms or water coolers in the work areas. We're doing it to be better at the business."

Conflict Between the Need to Change and Need for Security

"Change is a part of everyone's life," said Odom. "People want to change because that's the way they grow. Organizations change in order to remain viable. Businesses must change to be competitive. But in the middle of the need for change is the person's need for security and stability. So, you have a conflict.

"Recognizing this conflict, we developed a four-step management-of-change process to deal with a person's need for security as we introduced change.

"1) Assessment of your organization. As a leader, you need to know what the reaction is going to be to changing your organization. You can know this by knowing your people and the history of prior changes.

"2) Communication and information. In our traditional management style, management had all the information, which created problems between management and the workforce. The new thinking is that the way to get people comfortable with change is to communicate often and give them all the information that in the past only managers had.

"3) Involve your people in decisions. Especially involve the people affected by the change. In doing this, you build trust in the organization. We did this through our change design process. [See The Implementation Process at the end of this chapter.]

"4) Provide resources. You can't assume that management knows how to implement change. You have to bring in additional resources such as facilitators and consultants, and you have to spend a lot of time training people in the process of change.

"In each of these four steps, we keyed on the fact that we had to implement change to remain viable and competitive. At the same time, we always kept in front of us the fact that our people had a natural desire for stability."

Supervisors Had To Give Up Command-and-Control

Continued Odom, "Where did we get the most resistance from? It wasn't the workers. They'd been telling us for years that we weren't using them. It wasn't management; they wanted the change. It was the supervisors, because they felt they had a significant security problem. They thought, 'If teams are self-directed, what do we do?'

"We dealt with this by training a few supervisors to become facilitators. We told the other supervisors that we weren't eliminating their roles, but changing them, and here are examples of people we've done this with. The supervisors could see that they didn't have dead-end jobs. After we did this several times, supervisors began to buy in.

"We had said we wanted to eliminate the traditional supervisor and change them from the command-and-control person, to coach or facilitator," explained Odom. "The supervisors took us at our word and said they weren't going to tell people what to do anymore. But we were giving responsibility to workers who had never had it before and didn't know how to deal with it. So for a while, we felt as if we were in chaos.

"We had to say to supervisors, 'Let's make sure we understand what we mean when we say you're transitioning from supervisor to coach. It doesn't mean you just let go of the reins. Instead, you make sure your team knows what they're doing and then you gradually hand over the reins to them.'

"We've had some excellent results in fabrication. For example, in the traditional management style, we were running a four-shift operation, 24 hours a day, seven days a week with 280 people. And we were struggling to produce 3,000 wafers a month. With the new management style, we got equivalent throughput with a fifth of the people, using the same technology and specifications. Unfortunately, we've since closed the area because we have less military business."

Structure Is a Vital Part of the Change Effort

"Harris is unique in that we have a structure for our change process and for implementing SDWT's," said Ed Rose, production manager-turned-training manager. "The foundation was the four-step management-of-change process, which included our Implementation Process. There are also our Five Habits and our Awards Program.

"Before we began implementing SDWTs in our wafer fabrication module, we tried employee involvement teams. These were voluntary and worked on projects. But we changed to SDWTs because we needed teams with multi-functional skills. We still have aspects of employee involvement teams.

"We also created a new production-job family called fabrication technologist, which integrated production operator, engineering, and maintenance technicians into one job. In our wafer-fabrication facilities, the fabrication technologists took on all production, equipment, and process issues for their task. Manufacturing provided the content expertise, and human resources provided the human systems to support the changes.

"To form SDWTs, the members went through a six-step Developmental Process [see end of the chapter]. At first, we had team leaders, but this didn't work out. We were simply creating another level of management. So we moved to coordinators. In many ways this is the most powerful way to work because it's the shared responsibility concept. Individuals on the teams serve as coordinators for safety, production, training, administration, and projects/meetings. Teams add other coordinators as needed.

"The change to SDWTs had to occur via training, and the teams told us what they needed. We developed our training in four phases: forming, storming, norming, and performing, as defined by the Tuckman Model. It's done in one- to two-hour modules and is delivered to teams on their shifts. So, it also acts as team building. There are three skill categories: social, technical, and administrative.

"The heart of our training is to build a collaborative workforce, not a competitive one. Winning and losing is great for sporting events, but it has no place in interpersonal communication. Mutual respect is the foundation of human relations.

"When you implement SDWTs, basic behavior changes have to occur. In our case, many of our people had been with us 10 or 15 years, and we were trying to get them to do something totally foreign to them. Our feeling was that if we could change behaviors or habits, we would have a great base for a team to flourish. But to change a habit, you have to have knowledge, skill, and a desire to create a habit. We used Covey's *The Seven Habits of Highly Effective People* as a model for defining our five habits for successful team members. [See end of the chapter.]

"A significant part of our structure is our Team Excellence Awards Program. The criteria are based on the four phases of team development, six steps to SDWTs, and key plant metrics—on-time delivery, quality and factory cycle time. Area implementation teams can change the criteria to meet their internal needs.

"The awards system is based on trust. The team fills out an application saying they've completed the criteria and only the facilitator has to sign it. You can tell how an area is doing by the plaque on their wall. We have teams at different levels—bronze, silver, gold, but no platinum. That level is for teams who've gone through all the training and are doing everything that's outlined in the criteria. What Team Excellence Awards have done for us is beyond our wildest expectations."

The Change Was Like a Tug of War in the Beginning

"We started as a pilot team and didn't have guidelines, so it was like a madhouse," said Phyllis Davis, fabrication technologist. "Before we were a team, our supervisor would tell us what to do and our inputs weren't taken with importance.

"The change took a long time. The supervisors were concerned about their job security. It was a tug-of-war in the beginning both within the team and with support people, who didn't have any guidelines to direct us into the team environment. Everything was done by trial and error."

"Now we know the operations completely," said Sofia Davis, fabrication technologist. "Once the team got all the information, we began to look at things differently. For example, when we learned how much our gloves, chemicals, etc. cost, we realized how much money we were wasting and had more concern about the company's costs.

"Before, we hadn't understood about through-put yield, and on-time delivery. We now know that's what keeps us in business and have a better appreciation of management's burdens."

"In the past, the management was just someone you passed in the hallway," said Phyllis. "Today, they know who you are. Now, teams are a much better way to do our daily routines. Everyone has a coordinator role and we all know what we're doing."

"One thing we didn't understand at first were the reports," said Sofia. "We had to learn how to read the information. The supervisors became our 'suppliers,' giving us the information and training we needed to do this.

"In the past when we had a problem with a lot, we would have to put it on hold until an engineer could solve it. Sometimes the lot would sit for hours, or even days. After we were trained, when we caught a problem, we could solve it ourselves. Now it's an open door thing. If we have questions, we can telephone someone for assistance. In the past, we would have as many as 18 lots on hold. We've brought it down to one, which improved our cycle time tremendously.

"After awhile, we were no longer separate teams, but were communicating like one team across three shifts. For example, the team product coordinators all meet for a few minutes at the beginning and end of all shifts to discuss any equipment or lot problems."

"The work moves along better because everyone is working together for the same quality production goal," said Phyllis. "If an operator runs out of work, they'll help someone else. In the past, if product got scrapped, so what? Now, we want to investigate and know what scrapped it because it affects our company. If we're not making quality wafers, we're going to lose business."

"When we finally went over the hurdle, everything clicked and our team excelled," said Sofia. "And we were saving money. For example, we made a decision about some equipment we weren't using, but which was costing money just sitting idle. Our team presented all the dollars and cents to management. Team members came off their vacations and other people worked on their own time to prepare our presentation. It was 100% team involvement."

"Our sales people got excited because of what they saw and began bringing customers to us," said Phyllis. "Now we interface with our customers, sometimes in a round-table, or they'll call us direct. They'll show us what they want and we'll give them an estimated delivery date."

Watching People Grow is the Biggest Delight

"The team concept gives us self-esteem, because in the past we had a supervisor over us at all times," said Sofia. "Now we have an opportunity to have input on any given situation. We have ownership and can take pride in what we do. Our quality of work is better—and shows it.

"Teams are the way to go for the company to improve. But they have to have the right tools and training. And supervisors need to realize that they're suppliers for us and that we're not taking anything away from their positions."

"We couldn't have been self-directed teams without the training," said Phyllis. "Before, we were coming in and doing our eight hours and getting out. As we got into teams, we took pride in what we were doing. We were taught how to handle conflict and not point fingers, but to tell someone in a proper way about a problem. It took us a couple of years to learn to do this."

"One of the biggest delights I get from this change process is watching people grow," said Odom. "We have technologists who five years ago sat quietly in communication meetings. They were great workers but weren't letting themselves out. Now these same people can give a speech in front of a crowd of a thousand, telling about what their teams are doing. The improvement in the workers' self-esteem and their feelings about their abilities is a fantastic part of the process."

* * * * *

The Implementation Process

1. *"Sing from the same hymnal"* - Offer an off-site workshop that focuses on educating middle management on the concept of self-directed work teams and getting buy-in.
2. *Form a steering committee* - Create a committee to support and guide the change process.
3. *Form implementation teams* - Provide implementation flexibility within departments while coaching department employees through the change process.
4. *Provide management training* - Thoroughly educate middle management on self-directed work teams and interpersonal skills so they can lead the change process.
5. *Establish local training resources* - Provide training support in the form of facilities, training curricula, and facilitators to act as knowledge brokers to teams and management.
6. *Provide structure and guidance to teams* - Ensure that both

employees and managers demonstrate new competencies so that the new organization can succeed. They must believe one another to be trustworthy, skilled, and personally accountable.

Developmental Steps for Self-directed Work Teams

1. *Purpose* - Why do we exist as a team?
2. *Vision* - What do we want to look like in the future?
3. *Goals and Objectives* - What is the team trying to accomplish?
4. *Strategy/Tactics* - How will the team accomplish its goals and objectives?
5. *Roles and Responsibilities* - What tasks need to be done? Who will do them? What responsibilities need to be transferred to the team? When will they be transferred?
6. *Standards/Norms/Expectations* - What rules will guide our behaviors? How will the team handle conflicts?

Five Habits of Highly Effective Team Members

1. Understanding the need for a win/win interaction philosophy.
2. Mutual respect, including the development of an environment that will maintain and enhance team member self-esteem and allow the team to focus on problems and not personalities.
3. The need to be proactive.
4. The ability to listen with empathy.
5. The ability to appreciate differences in personalities and opinions.

Date of Case Study: October 1994

1997 Epilogue: Ed Rose reports that in the two years that have elapsed, "More than 30 companies have come to benchmark our teams. The teams are progressing nicely on their journeys; all have advanced beyond the bronze phase and are at least in the silver phase; some are working on gold. And we've enhanced our team training with an experiential learning course and delivery of both the Theory of Constraints and Zodiac, The Game of Business Finance & Strategy created by Paradigm Learning of Tampa, Florida. Like a mechanic, a team is only as good as the tools it uses.

"We're also involved with the University of North Texas on a research project, funded by the National Science Foundation with eight other U.S. companies participating. From this, we expect to learn how to use high performance team concepts in our white collar environments, while focusing on leadership and training."

Ray Odom continues as plant manager; Ed Rose has been appointed as Harris Semiconductor's corporate practice expert on self-directed work teams and is writing *Training and Presenting With Magic,* to be published by McGraw Hill in June, 1997.

23

At AAL, Teams Continue to Pay Off After Seven Years

One of the first service organizations to implement self-managed work teams, Aid Association for Lutherans is more than maintaining the transformation begun in 1987.

PROFILE

Organization: Aid Association for Lutherans, a fraternal benefit society founded in 1902.
Members: 1.6 million, including Lutherans and their families.
Services: Life insurance, disability and long-term care insurance, retirement products. Affiliates offer mutual funds and credit union services.
Assets: About $12.8 billion under management.
Employees: 2,400 field personnel; 1,800 full-time and regular part-time home office personnel.
Headquarters: Appleton, Wisconsin

* * * * *

Seven years ago, Aid Association for Lutherans, financially one of the strongest insurance companies in the U.S., began a transformation that seemed impossible for a service organization. The company followed the lead of the manufacturing sector and dared to take, what was for them, the courageous step of implementing self-managed work teams. At the time, such teams had been virtually untested in the service sector.

Unlike some other businesses that had undergone dramatic change, AAL was not acting out of immediate concern for survival. But in the long view, Richard Gunderson, AAL's President and CEO since 1985, could read the signs: increasing competition, lower margins and, in spite of new automation, stagnating productivity. He and others in AAL's top management realized changes were needed if the company was to maintain its good health.

Focusing on reengineering AAL's structure, work style and culture, the company's new approach produced remarkable results. In less than three years, one department saw a 20% increase in productivity, a reduction of case processing time by as much as 75%, and the staff trimmed by about 150 positions—the majority by attrition.

During the first year of the transformation, AAL's largest department, Insurance Products Services, reduced the number of supervisor positions from 62 to 22 and eliminated about 58 full-time jobs and three layers of supervision. At the same time, their work volume increased 10 percent.

As one part of AAL's transformation, nearly 500 Insurance Products Services employees at corporate headquarters organized into 17 self-managed work teams comprised of about 20-30 multi-skilled employees. Each team is part of a group that serves one of the company's four regional areas and performs all the tasks needed to underwrite a new policy, change an existing policy, or process an insurance claim. The teams do their own hiring, training, and vacation-scheduling.

Transformations such as AAL's are impressive and generate tremendous excitement when they're begun. But can they be maintained? Jeffrey R. Hahn, second vice president, Insurance Services, North Central Region, talked about how AAL is building on its gains since it took its brave step into radical change.

Getting Used To Never-ending Change

"Looking back, it seems like just yesterday that people were piling things on their chairs and rolling them to their new work areas," recalled Hahn. "We've come a long way since then and feel pretty good about our progress. But we also have a sense of opportunities ahead and how far we have yet to go.

"There's a constant challenge to keep fresh and not slip back into old habits. The job is never done. We use the term 'journey' to describe what we're doing because adapting to change is an ongoing process.

"There's a growing sense of appreciation that what we did was necessary. People are realizing that change is going to be a constant with us, rather than that our transformation is settling down, is done with, or that we're going back to the way things were."

Key Measures Tell if AAL is Still on Track: Productivity, Customer Satisfaction, Internal Satisfaction

"One of the things that changed in our new way of working was people's awareness of how well they were doing their jobs," continued Hahn. "In the past, we had tracked everything and had lots of data. People got plenty of direct feedback on how much they did, not necessarily on how well they did it. This feedback is pretty easy to give when you have a limit to your job.

"But when we changed to our team structure, we eliminated a lot of informational systems because we thought it was more important that employees change the way they work rather than track things all the time.

"But we left employees in the lurch because they didn't really know if they were doing a good job. There weren't any measures. So we've been rebuilding our measures over time.

"One key measure we use to let us know how we're doing is a productivity measure that looks at what we do and what it costs. From 1986-1992, we saw a 40% cumulative increase in productivity. Of course, the gains in the first year or two were significant because of the shift to teams.

"But we've been able to maintain an annual 2-3% productivity improvement since then. And now we're looking at implementing some major technology such as imaging and expert systems that will give us even more gains.

"I think we're on the brink of seeing some pretty significant performance improvement increases.

"Another important measure is internal customer satisfaction. We have a professional field staff of 2,400 men and women across the country who work directly with our members. They sit across the table from some of our families and help meet their financial needs. So we look at the field staff as our internal customers.

"We initially surveyed the field staff twice a year and have seen some pretty significant improvements. In 1985, only 27% of the field staff agreed or strongly agreed that Insurance Products Services understood the field staff. In 1991, we were up to 60%.

"Our service methodology is built around Leonard Berry's five measures of customer satisfaction: 1) Tangibleness, meaning the equipment, the physical environment, how people dress, the image, etc.; 2) Reliability, the ability to perform dependably and consistently; 3) Responsiveness, timely and prompt service; 4) Assurance, how knowledgeable are the employees and do they convey a sense of trust to customers; 5) Empathy, which has to do with how they take care of people, being sympathetic and caring and giving individualized attention.

"A third area we track is employee satisfaction. We've always known intuitively that this is an integral part of being a strong company and communication is particularly important. In 1985, only 40% of our employees agreed that communication is important between us and our customers. In 1991, 69% agreed.

"Another area in which we've improved is in people's perception that they're being challenged to be innovative on the job. From 1987 to 1991, this improved from 58% to 69%.

"Our surveys also have shown a downside. In 1987, only 67%

of our employees agreed that they had had adequate advance training to do the work. In the transformation, we had asked them to step into new roles and do new things. They want to do a good job and when they don't feel equipped, they're uncomfortable."

Four Keys to Maintaining Transformation

"In maintaining our transformation, we're focusing on training, compensation, performance management, and continuous improvement," said Hahn. "Seven years ago, the first thing we looked at was training. This was needed if we were going to operate in a team environment with multi-skilled employees who face off with customers. You need a whole different skill set and approach to work.

"We developed an internal training program we call Flex-Team Training. It has a number of modules we roll out over 18 months. These take people through a set of individual skills all the way from customer focus to service excellence.

"We designed a module that simulates the life of our district representatives—our field sales people. We also worked with a personal profile instrument to help people understand their personality styles and how these would help or hinder them on a team.

"In addition, we looked at team development, using the National Training Labs' model of forming, storming, norming, and performing teams. And we focused on leadership and followership.

"We keep reinforcing the training because if you introduce a subject just once, it's like a basic college 101 course. You understand some of the words, but you certainly don't know how to apply them. You learn just enough to pass the test. We don't want to just pass the test. We want to be world class in all we do.

"To support this, we have the Employee Development Council, which is responsible for setting direction for employee development. It's made up of technical specialists, managers, and team members. This group is shaping, assessing, and partnering with our Human Resources Department in delivering training on an ongoing basis. Our training is continuous because we realized we needed to make more of an investment in people as a critical resource of the organization."

Compensation Based on Department Performance

"After our organizational change, we were working in a different way, but our compensation system was unchanged," continued Hahn. "We saw that this had to be modified also.

"Like some other companies, we looked at a Pay-for-Knowledge system. The philosophy behind this is that the more people know, the better they're going to serve your customers. But what you run into is that there are business needs and limitations. And if you don't use a skill often enough, you're not sharp at it. Also, sometimes people learn things they don't need.

"So, we designed a Pay-for-Applied-Services system. People have to be certified not only that they're technically competent in skills, but that the skill is needed on their team.

"Pay-for-Applied-Services looks at skill blocks, which are the employees' personal assignments or job descriptions. These tend to be based on tasks such as life insurance, disability insurance, underwriting, claims, billing, address changes, etc. We aggregate these skills and, through a grid, develop a base pay, which is one element of our compensation.

"A second element is Individual Incentive Compensation, which recognizes the stars—those high-level performers who exceed expectations. They're eligible for annual incentive bonuses based on their contribution to the success of the operation.

"A third element is team/departmental performance. A portion of their compensation is an annual bonus based on the success of their department. We've finely tuned this. In the beginning, we had a concept of 'friendly competition' among teams and based compensation on team results, but we found this was sub-optimizing the organization.

"The commitment and caring of our employees is such that if we get off track, they send us signals; and if we take some organizational barriers out of their way, some pretty neat things happen.

They told us team competition was getting in the way of doing a good job for the company. They said, 'It doesn't make any sense to compete with each other.' So as of last year, the team incentive compensation is the same percentage for all teams, based on AAL's and IPS' overall performance.

"Our corporate gainsharing, which we call Success Share, is another type of compensation. All employees are rewarded according to the results of the entire operation.

"Altogether, this means that we have variable compensation that focuses on productivity and customer satisfaction. We can't afford to routinely annuitize salary increases every year forever."

Performance Management Includes 360-degree Feedback

Continued Hahn, "Some people ask, 'Why do you need managers when you have self-managing teams? Isn't that an oxymoron?' It's really not. In this structure, managers have some key roles, such as coaching, counseling, and performance management.

"We've always done a pretty good job with performance reviews and helping people understand how they're doing. But we've made some changes, one of which includes how we assess team performance. Basically, we do this through outcome measures, rather than just telling everybody they're doing a good job.

"We've also made some strides in 360-degree feedback. In our old model of performance appraisal, your boss would call you in once a year and tell you how you were doing. In our 360-degree model, the manager and direct report play a key role in the discussion. But people provide information about their own performance, and the manager, peers, and subordinates also give input. So there's a much greater perspective on performance. We still have individual performance appraisals, and that's a key role for managers.

"A lot of self-managing takes place in our teams and service groups. Originally, we had service boundaries, which we call Service Clouds. Our vision was that these would eventually blur and mesh, and we've seen that happen. People can be asked to do many different things. So 'It's not in my job description' doesn't get mentioned much around here.

"What used to happen was that people who were good technicians were moved into management positions. And if you were dealing with our field staff and didn't like an answer you received, you bumped the decision up to someone higher. And someone at the top would basically overrule and make the call on the case.

"That tended to happen when we first moved into teams. But what people got back from the manager or director was something like, 'What did the underwriter say? I'm not an underwriter. And I have a lot of confidence in the people making the decisions.'

"Now, very few decisions get bumped up. And when they do, that's where the manager's role comes in. He or she manages across organizational boundaries and brings in a broader business perspective. As a result, we're also seeing a broader business perspective on the part of teams, which they're bringing into account as they make daily decisions.

"Our teams run the day-to-day business. And one of our interesting challenges as we further refine the self-managing effort is to understand the role of managers in identifying processes for teams to improve."

Getting More Serious About Quality

"While the IPS department has made great strides through the use of teams, AAL as a whole has looked at how we leverage the gains in IPS and across the organization by being more deliberate about Total Quality Management," continued Hahn. "When we began our transformation corporately, we chose not to focus on quality. We believed we were a quality organization. Looking at conventional measures, we were the top one or two in the industry in almost everything. We were rock solid financially and felt very good about that. But we didn't understand quality from the 'Big Q' perspective—a focus on the customer, continuous improvement, process orientation and the like.

"Early in the 1990s, we decided we needed to get more serious about quality. In focusing on marketing, we realized there was more to knowing and meeting our customers' needs than we knew about. We also saw that we could be more disciplined.

"We worked with Bill Golomski, a past judge for the Malcolm Baldrige National Quality Award, and he led us in a self-appraisal based on Baldrige criteria. As a nonprofit organization, we're not eligible for the Baldrige. But it was a framework we could use to try to understand where our organization was.

"We came into the appraisal with fairly high expectations but scored less than 300 out of a possible 1000 points. That opened a few eyes. We were doing a lot of things well, but not in deliberate ways. We had a commitment and passion for stewardship, but it wasn't formalized or done in a systematic way.

"So, we had the Juran Institute help us look at improving quality in the organization, not as another program but as a way to change the way we do business. These past few years, we've been learning about quality and setting up some higher efforts around improvement, planning, and managing business processes.

"Corporately, we're putting in place the infrastructure to help us use quality as the way we do business. With our service teams, we had a great framework for working on quality improvement. But we wanted to make sure we understood such things as quality principles. We have five basic principles: 1) Lead from the top; 2) Act on fact; 3) Focus on the customer; 4) Empower and respect people; 5) Continuously improve.

"We also created a definition of quality: 'Quality is ever more improved processes, ever more improved products, ever more caring relationships all of which give delight to ever more customers year after year.'

"This year, we've begun some quality pilot projects to help us in our team environment to understand our customers' expectations and change our processes on a day-to-day basis.

"Our efforts in IPS are complementary to things happening at the corporate level. In the past four years, we've had a productivity improvement program and recognition and have seen some significant dollar savings.

"Now, among other things, we're looking at how to retain the sense of moving ahead by focusing on Best Practices, rather than everyone doing their own thing. Instead of convincing employees to adopt the best practices, it's up to them to prove why practices that have been demonstrated to be effective in other departments won't work for them."

Lessons Learned

"We can tell people who are considering changing their organization that it can be done. It's not just theoretical," said Hahn.

"One lesson we learned was that you can make some pretty dramatic changes in an organization and still have fun. As we went along, a celebration committee helped us recognize the milestones.

"We also learned that people have power to change themselves. Early in the process, someone came to my office in tears about the change process and didn't want to go through it. A year later, she was bubbling about what she had learned. She felt very confident and self-assured. So the idea that people can change is important.

"Along with this is the concept of patient persistence. While we know change is inevitable, growth is optional. Being persistent and realizing there are ebbs and flows in the pace of change and that you do make progress along the way is pretty important.

"We also learned that no matter how much we thought we were communicating and explaining to help people understand, we weren't doing enough. You can never give too much information. And the flip side is, you can never listen too much. If you listen to people, even if you don't like what they're saying, very often you'll discover a nugget of truth.

"The key changes you need to make are with your management team. They need to be open to looking at things in a new way.

"Finally, the organization's people and their understanding of the customers and their desire to do the right thing is a very powerful force to tap into. This force and the role of the manager in coaching, counseling, and shaping that raw energy and initiative into a focus on your business goals and your customers is really a neat combination."

Date of Case Study: March, 1994

1997 Epilogue: Jeff Hahn's predictions about the inevitability of change and the need for persistence have been realized during the intervening three years at AAL. "Our teams have continued to change, both in terms of nature and size," he said. "In our service operation, we have fewer, larger teams, and we've brought more functions into the service teams.

"At the same time, we've done some things that have moved us in a more traditional direction. We've moved away from our pay for applied services system, because we found that the complexity was starting to burden us too much. We've gone back to a whole job concept where we have formal job descriptions and pay grades linked to those job descriptions.

"We're also using different kinds of teams. We continue to have self-managing work teams covering broad areas, but we're also using more teams with a project focus; more and more people have longer-term assignments rather than defined jobs. And we're learning about using teams in different ways for different purposes.

"Teams will be key to our future. We'll use virtual teams and dispersed teams as well as intact work groups—teams that are of long duration and those that are project-based and working on specific tasks with a finite life cycle. We'll continue to refine and focus our measurement, we'll use groupware to support the virtual teams, and the role of team management will continue to evolve.

"The financial services industry continues to undergo tremendous change. The competitive environment has changed. Consumers are changing in their demands. Part of our response is to become more nimble and responsive. Teams help us do that."

24

Vision, Customer Focus and Teams: Recipe for Success at Tennalum

First, the success part of this story. Since 1991:
- Total production for the facility is up 50%
- Market share is up 50%
- The customer retention rate is at 100%
- Revenues are up 102%
- Gross profits are up 280%
- Workers compensation costs are down 96%

If that's not attention-getting enough, here are more results:
- Promise performance has averaged more than 98% for the last five years
- Claim-free performance has averaged more than 99.5% for the same period
- Bonuses, which are available to all regular employees except the plant manager and sales/marketing manager, have averaged more than 10% since the plan started in 1993
- 1% turnover

And there's been a lot of third-party recognition along the way, including:
- Recipient of the Shingo Prize for Excellence in Manufacturing
- 21st Century Organizational Excellence Award, sponsored by Clemson University

- One of *Industry Week* magazine's 25 finalists for "Best Operating Plant"
- TOP (Top Operations and Plants) Award by 33 Metal Producing Magazine
- Tennessee Quality Award (1994, 1995, 1996; based on the Malcolm Baldrige National Quality Award criteria)
- Recipient of the Madison Award which focuses on local community relations
- ISO 9002 Registration

* * * * *

This is a case study about vision, customer focus and self-directed teams. It's also a story about leadership, change management and culture. In other words, it's about the "soft stuff" that got those hard results.

We'll hear the story from Tennalum's Vice President and General Manager, Larry Swick, and the facility's Organizational Development Manager, Jeff Salyer. They have been key players since Tennalum began its growth in 1992.

A division of Kaiser Aluminum, Tennalum employs 214 non-union people in four rotating shifts at its 290,000 (soon to be 315,000) square foot Jackson, Tennessee facility. The facility extrudes aluminum alloy raw materials into various sized and shaped rods and bars from which its automotive and aerospace end users manufacture 4,200 different products. Eighty to 85 percent of Tennalum's output is sold through metal distributors on a make-to-order basis. There is only one U.S. competitor in its specialty market. Sales were $90 million in 1996.

It Took a Vision

"Following a very difficult two and a half year startup time, we decided in 1992 to sit down and decide who we were, what we were and how we were going to go about doing business," said Larry Swick. "We were strongly influenced by Joel Barker's videotape, 'The Power of Vision.'

"During a lot of serious discussion by our core staff group, off-site, we came up with our vision concepts and a symbolic representation of our vision of the business. It's a triangle that has three sides, Preferred Supplier, Preferred Employer and Preferred Investment. It's an equilateral triangle, because all three are equally important.

"Customers, employees and resources are, of course, the three primary components needed by all businesses. We put our customers on the base of the triangle for a particular reason: you don't have a business without customers. We also knew we couldn't get and maintain customers unless we had an excellent cadre of employees to get the task done; and without resources it's difficult to get up a head of steam.

"But it wasn't enough to just say that we wanted to be the preferred supplier, employer and investment. We realized we needed a set of criteria for each, so if we accomplished those things we would indeed be the preferred supplier, preferred employer and preferred investment.

"What we said we have to do to be the preferred supplier," continued Swick, "is:
- meet or exceed customer expectations
- deliver on time, every time
- have zero claims
- have consistent products that always look and perform better than the competition's
- offer competitively priced products
- provide superior support and service
- be responsive by being accessible, resolving complaints promptly and having quick, accurate order entry—which was where saw we could get a competitive advantage and was a primary reason that our sales through distribution have gone from 40% in 1991 to 82% last year
- be the easiest to do business with, the most flexible
- guarantee everything we do—if you don't like our product, you can ship it back to us; and, no, our customers don't take advantage of us, which is hard to do if you provide a quality product that they want, when they want it and at a competi-

tive price
- offer the shortest lead times, and
- be continuously improving—which to us means that every day, every time we do something, we need to think about how we can do it better today than we did it yesterday.

"Of course, we tested these criteria with our customers and throughout our organization. After we got buy-in from everybody that these were the right things to work on, we went about working on them.

"On the preferred employer side, we said we needed to:
- offer competitive salaries and benefits
- offer secure employment—no layoffs, which we've avoided during the valleys by working on our capital projects and stepping up the pace of our training
- be responsive to employee needs—our PEST team, Preferred Employer Steering Team, made up of technician representatives from our operating teams, meets once a month and is free to recommend policies in all areas except salaries and benefits
- provide a clean and safe workplace
- use self-directed work teams—our way of getting at empowerment, responsibility and accountability
- have effective communications flowing both ways, and
- have growth opportunities—since there are only three levels in this facility [technicians in the production, maintenance and administrative areas, a core group of 20 staff, and the VP/general manager], we've had to make sure people have opportunities to grow their skill and knowledge capabilities within their jobs.

"The third leg of the triangle is Preferred Investment. The criteria on that are:
- be the low cost producer
- exceed our return on EBIT targets [Earnings Before Interest and Taxes]

- exceed plan performance—business plan, safety plan, monthly plan, exceed all plan performance
- explore and develop new alloys and new products—we commit a percentage of our total revenue to this, and
- consistently expand market opportunities.

"We involved everybody in the organization in developing our vision, which included about 110 people in 1992. We started with a core group of staff folks, took a cross-section of 50 people offsite, then took every team in the facility offsite to work through the triangle and the criteria to get understanding and buy-in.

"This was all very important to our shifting from being a cost center to becoming a profit center in 1992. It really helped us bring focus to what we had to do to be a successful, growing business.

"Our vision was the first step toward our future. In 1993, we developed a five year strategic plan, which originated from the vision. That's one of Joel Barker's essential points: that you can't do strategic planning without having a vision of what your business is all about. Annually, we develop an operating plan, which causes us to test the vision every year. But our principles and core values are all rolled up together in the vision and it's stood the test of time so far.

"And we've been very pleased with the results we've gotten by adhering to our vision and following our strategic plan."

It Also Takes a Positive Culture

"As a business, instead of a cost center," said Jeff Salyer, "we realized we needed to do some investing in our people. The old saying is true, that 'you need to spend money to make money.'

"In the two and a half year startup period, we really underestimated what we would have to spend and how long it would take for our self-directed work teams to mature. Our people were mostly locally hired and came out of traditional organizations. They not only had to learn a new production operation, but at the same time had to learn a new organizational concept, the self-directed work team approach.

"The cornerstones of the self-directed teams were put in place during the startup, creating the foundation for our growth in the 90's. Members of the original startup team still at Tennalum are John Cole, Mark Lane, Tom Dixon, Glenn Willis, led by Roy Coates and later supplemented by Harry Hoffman and myself.

"After Larry arrived in 1992 and we'd developed our vision and the criteria for each side of the triangle, it became a lot clearer what we needed to do. In addition to focusing on understanding our customers' requirements, creating the best products and value for them, having excellent internal process capabilities, providing a safe working environment and performing preventive maintenance religiously, we've also been emphasizing our TEAM attitude for continuous improvement [Together Everybody Achieves More], providing eight hours of team and skill training for our teams every quarter, and we're using a pay-for-skills system, which is a cross-training system that gives team members the flexibility to move to any spot on the line where they're needed.

"We've worked hard at developing a culture of trust. We have no supervisors at this facility. There is no management on off shifts. Team members make the final decisions on product quality and can shut down the equipment if there are safety or quality problems. There are no fences, guards or designated parking, except for handicapped spaces. Everybody has a key to the front door, which doesn't mean as much now that we have a 24-hour, seven day a week operation. This is just a different view of the world, where trust is important and very rarely backfires on you.

"The whole facility is salaried, with the team members being non-exempt—which means they are paid overtime, and they are paid if they're sick or have family problems and are unable to be here. We feel that's part of being the preferred employer."

Asked how the facility handles absenteeism abuses, Larry Swick responded, "Our expectation is no more than 2% absenteeism. We let everyone know what our overall absenteeism is running and we let every team know what the absenteeism rate is on their team. It's their responsibility to address the problem if there is one. We also recognize and reward perfect attendance."

"Handling absenteeism is a relatively easy concept for teams to understand and handle," continued Salyer. "They know if someone isn't there who should be, that makes it tougher for everyone on the team because we don't replace people who are absent. Team members also know absenteeism negatively affects their bonus, because when people are absent we don't make as much product as we could and we also make an adjustment to individual bonuses for absenteeism.

"On a more positive note, we have a lot of celebrations for accomplishments. We'll have one soon to celebrate 1996 results, the Tennessee Quality Award, a record shipment month in January and record profits. We usually have some kind of a food event and gifts for everybody. Sometimes family members attend and we have local news media in to report the event. It's important that people feel they had a part in our accomplishments and that they know they're appreciated."

Self-Direction at Work

"We have three types of teams at Tennalum—process teams, slice teams and project teams," continued Salyer.

"Process teams are the same thing as self-directed work teams. They're natural work groups that have a interdependency because they work on equipment together, or the equipment they work on affects the person downstream from them. It's the process teams that produce the aluminum bars and rods that we manufacture. And they do it without supervision, as we've already said.

"We've taken the low key approach on team leaders for the process teams. Our team leaders are not pseudo supervisors. The team picks the team leader. That individual is responsible for the team meeting agenda, for leading the team meetings and for reviewing time sheets to make sure they're administratively correct. The team decides on whether and when the team leader responsibility is rotated.

"It is not up to the team leader to ride herd on the team. All team members are trained to do their jobs and they're empowered to take whatever action they feel is appropriate in a given situation.

"As for team accountability, if there's a serious problem on the team and management has to step in, we get the whole team together to talk about it and to come up with a corrective action and a way to keep it from happening again. We tell the teams that they need to come up with a solution or management will."

"Some people suggest that this does away with individual responsibility," interjected Swick. "Nothing could be further from the truth. In our facility, the individual is responsible *to* the team and the team is responsible *for* the individual. Instead of management going to the individual, it's the team that handles the problem. The individual still has to be a responsible member of the team and of this organization."

"We've learned that it's important for management to set the boundaries for what teams can do and what they can't do," continued Salyer. "And when something is outside the boundaries, management needs to step in and say that's not okay. Teams are not a democracy. As leaders, we have a responsibility to run the business. Having a self-directed/teaming organization never means that you abdicate your responsibility for leadership. Our handbook stipulates certain actions that will be taken in extreme cases such as fighting, drugs and bringing certain things onto the premises. And, yes, teams do schedule their own vacations.

"Communications are important, of course. Teams overlap a half hour to talk about things that carry over from shift to shift. Each work center is on line and has access to work procedures, special instructions and quality procedures. A lot of the traditional things are built into the system.

"As for hiring, we use three standardized tests and put candidates through a behavioral interview and an assessment center, then they're hired and sent to the teams to decide which team they go on. In our environment, hiring the right people is critical, and it's important that if they don't work out they be cut loose."

Added Swick, "I recently heard someone say at a conference that you're making a million dollar decision on each new hire. That's full cost for an employee at $50,000 for 20 years. It tells you how critical a decision this is."

"Not to mention the impact that that person can have on your plant," continued Salyer. "After hiring, we have a peer review at 30, 60 and 90 days using pre-set criteria. After that, a person can be reviewed by the team at any time that there's a performance issue, an attitude problem or anything else that needs attention.

"Our compensation system has three parts: basic pay, pay for skills and the bonus plan. Everybody starts at an entry level salary and learns sets of skills during three approximately six month periods. There are written and demonstration tests after each skills learning period. After eighteen months to two and a half years, they're topped out on basic pay and pay for skills.

"Our home-grown bonus plan starts as soon as technicians are hired. It's paid out monthly as a percentage of their gross pay earned and is based primarily on the plant's return on assets and on high [99%+] promise performance and claim-free performance. If we don't make money in a month, nobody gets a bonus; but if we make more money, the bonus increases. We've had two months when no bonus was paid, the highest payout was 18-1/2% and the average has been 10% over the past three years. It was about 11-1/2% in 1996. Our bonus system is a constant reminder of our goals and successes. The two most critical things affecting the thinking of our people are our vision/direction and our bonus system."

Slice and Project Teams

"Next, we have the slice teams," said Salyer, "which means there's one person on them from each process team, for at least a year, picked by the process team. They meet once a month anywhere from two hours to eight hours, and there's no extra compensation for being on them.

"Slice teams are planning and tactics oriented or are very specialized in what it is they're trying to do. Our standing slice teams are safety, quality, PEST, ISO 9002 and training. They each have specific things to work on and have outputs. For example, in the safety area we have a sub team that developed and does our ergonomics training.

"We have a series of manuals that were completely developed by the slice teams—on ergonomics, accident prevention, three-year safety plans—that are updated annually. A lot of our facility policies are discussed in slice team meetings.

"We don't call them committees, because committees typically meet and meet but don't do anything. Teams have results. That's one of our cultural norms, to not use the word 'committee.'

"The third type is project teams, sometimes called task forces in other organizations. They're problem-solving and improvement oriented, and are formed and disbanded as needed. Examples include our LOMA process improvement team, teams that are formed to plan our celebrations and picnics, and when we upgraded our systems we formed a team to come up with the strategy and plan. Some of them last a month, some last six months and then they go away."

Leadership Style

"There is a style to this kind of organization. As I said, this isn't a democracy; it's participative. Teams make the operating decisions, but management still has the responsibility and accountability for the business.

"Trust is so essential in this culture. It's hard to build and so easy to tear down, but you just need to keep going. "

"It's like the three most important rules in real estate—location, location and location," interjected Swick. "I would say that the three most important rules for this kind of organization are trust, trust and trust."

"We find ways to get the technicians involved—in the production and the administrative areas—such as on special assignments in training, safety or quality. And then there's the general team emphasis, empowerment, continuous improvement and capability improvement which we mentioned earlier."

Added Swick, "You cannot improve the overall capability of your organization, without improving the capabilities of the members of your organization. Conversely, I believe that anything you put into improving the capabilities of your people will automatically upgrade the capabilities of the organization. That's the basis for our training concepts and anything we do to upgrade the skills and knowledge's of our people."

"A lot of these things are mind-set issues," said Salyer. "You just have to keep thinking that way as you do your day-to-day and week-to-week business.

"We do have specific roles for leadership. Of course, the first one is the obligation to establish the vision and to test it with your people. We needed to do that to facilitate the growth we've seen in the past four years. As with the chicken and the egg, we're not sure which comes first, the vision or the growth, but they both happened in 1992. Now, when everyone has a decision to make, it's the vision they check that decision against—which decision, A or B, will get us closer to being the preferred supplier, the preferred employer or the preferred investment?

"Another role is that management is a resource, not a supervisor. We're with the teams every day to help them solve their problems. Our emphasis is on coaching and facilitation. Coaches call plays. Rarely does a coach tell a team 'Do what you want to do and it'll be okay.' But in the heat of the action, coaches don't tell the players how to play.

"As managers, we avoid decision making on routine process problems. Instead, we ask, 'What would you do?' Ninety percent of the time they know what they want to do, they're just looking for somebody to confirm it. After awhile they don't ask because they get confidence in themselves that they can make the right decisions.

"And management is responsible for putting a focus on training, including skills training and the tools of self-management. You can't assume that people know how teams are supposed to work, what their responsibilities are and about the tools at their disposal.

"Our organization chart shows the process teams at the top, and the staff team—including the plant manager—at the bottom. Among the staff team is a group that Larry calls the Strategy Team, which runs the day-to-day business; it includes the sales and marketing manager, the plant engineering manager, the plant controller/administrator, the quality manager, the operations manager, the business manager and the organizational development manager. Our people in the plant are making the product and adding value to it. We believe staff's role is to do whatever we need to do to support that."

Added Swick, "It may seem like a small thing, but I believe it's been real important to constantly reinforce that we're a non-traditional organization. Not that you have to be non-traditional to be successful, but that being non-traditional has helped us be successful.

"As for the awards we've received, we use the application processes as a substitute for benchmarking. The application processes really test your organization; we learn from them ideas on how we can get better. And awards are a very good marketing tool; you can market the fact that you're putting your organization through these kinds of things so you can serve customers better. Some awards require you to set up systems to continually audit your processes, thereby encouraging continuous improvement."

Asked why Tennalum adopted its management style and has applied the concept of empowerment in the way it has, Salyer responded with a fable:

"Every morning in Africa, a gazelle wakes up and knows it must run faster than the fastest lion or it will be killed.

Also every morning in Africa, a lion wakes up and knows it must outrun the slowest gazelle or it will starve to death.

So it doesn't matter whether you're a lion or a gazelle, one thing is for sure: when the sun comes up, you'd better be running.

"That sums up the philosophy we try to instill here—that you can't just rest on your laurels; you've got to keep moving. You've got to have ceaseless focus on the customer and marketplace, endless emphasis on empowerment and continuous improvement, continuous exploitation of the strengths of your culture, constant development of your products and processes, and full utilization of your main resources—people, technology and capital. There's always somebody nipping at your heels."

Date of Case Study: February, 1997

Appendix 1

Management Style—A Quick Self-Assessment

This assessment provides a way to take a quick "thermometer" reading of Total Quality Management maturity in an organization, and whether leadership or traditional management is prevalent in that organization. (As with a real thermometer, this tool has its limitations; a full assessment using more comprehensive diagnostic tools may be in order.)

It has been a particularly powerful tool when administered to groups of managers who have little awareness of TQM and the elements of leadership. It often reveals that there is a major gap between current and desired levels of performance. It, therefore, gives managers an awareness that improvement is both needed and possible in their organization. It can also be used to check progress when scores are compared with an earlier assessment to learn if and how much the gap has closed.

Here is how this assessment tool is usually administered in connection with TQM and management style awareness education:

1. Attendees are asked to check the box, in each of the seven vertical columns, which most closely describes their organization's situation.
2. The attendees' individual assessments are then combined by counting the total number of check marks in each box.
3. Next, the total number of check marks in each box is multiplied by the appropriate point value on the left edge of the matrix (1, 2, 3, 4 or 5).
4. The multiplied figures in each vertical column/element are then added together and divided by the total number of check marks in that column.
5. The result is an average point value (such as 1.7) which expresses the group's perception of their organization's TQM maturity in each of the seven columns.
6. To compute point values (maturity) for each of the four major leadership elements, average the point values for the appropriate columns (two columns each for Lead, Empower, Assess, and one for Partner).

A lively discussion usually follows presentation of the results to the attendees, focusing on why the organization scored the way it did in each element and what might be done to improve.

Management Style—

TQM Element / Status Level	Leadership and Support	Strategic Planning	Employee Training and Recognition
5 (Desired Direction ↑)	Senior Managers personally and visibly involved. TQ culture permeates organization. Active removal of barriers. Policies and practices are aligned.	Planning effort is integrated, cross-functional and organization wide. Action plans developed at all levels. Customer needs are a primary planning tool.	All trained in and using TQ. Innovative incentive systems. Comprehensive systematic training.
4	Senior Managers participate in key activities. Departments cooperate. Managers held accountable for quality. Aligning policies and practices.	Action plans at most levels. Customer needs are a significant factor in planning. Many planning participants from across the organization.	Nearly all using TQ methods. Team achievements widely celebrated.
3	Senior Managers fully support TQ. Adequate resources invested. Some cross-functional implementation.	Action plans developed in key mission areas. Broad participation. Customer needs influence planning.	Almost all trained in TQ. Recognition of teams for continuous improvement efforts. Significant training resources.
2	Many Managers support TQ. Numerous improvement projects underway. Cross-functional implementation encouraged. Vision and values written	Specific goals established. Customer needs are considered in planning. Some participation from across the organization.	Managers and some employees trained in TQ. Some rewards for quality improvements. Some training resources.
1	Some managers support TQ. Some resources allocated, but few projects underway. Starting to organize and plan improvement effort.	General goals established. Customer needs are not central to goal-setting. Not an integrated effort.	Minimal training resources. Trainaing at TQ awareness level. Mostly managers. Occasional recognition given.

A Quick Self-Assessment

ower	Assess		Partner	
Employee Empowerment and Teamwork	**Continuous Improvement and Analysis**	**Continuous Quality Assurance Activity**	**Customers and Partners**	
Participative management the norm. Short chain-of-command. Employee enthusiasm apparent. Self directed teams functioning.	Continuous improvement progress tracked in all areas. Process floor-time and costs down in all areas.	Exceptional results from continual assessment and benchmarking of all products, services.	Innovative methods for obtaining customer feedback. Partnerships established to support continuous improvement.	D E G R E E O F L I N E I N V O L V E M E N T
Widespread participative management and downward delegation. Team ownership of process improvement.	Continuous improvement progress tracked in most areas. Process flow-time and costs down in key areas.	Positive performance trends from systematic assessment. Benchmarking for comparison.	Effective feedback system for obtaining customer information and improving services.	
Participative management style. Trust growing between managers and employees.	Quality data often used to track progress and identify problems/solutions. Some improvements noted.	Assessment of all products, services for outside customers and most for internal customers.	Customer feedback regularly solicitied for management action. Supplier quality monitored.	
Many managers support teams. Many employees on teams. More cross-functional cooperation.	Some units collect and analyze quality data to prevent errors. Beginning process and product improvement.	Most products, services for outside customers are reviewed. Positive results.	Customer feedback solicited on an ad hoc basis. Supplier performance not systematically tracked.	
Few quality improvement teams. Traditional management style. Little cross-functional cooperation.	Quality control by inspection or review. Quality data scarce. Feedback system in planning stage.	Some products, services reviewed to meet cusatomr needs.	Customer complaints are primary method of feedback and not systematically used to improve processes.	

This is an adaptation of a benchmarking tool developed by NASA Johnson Space Center and KPMG Peat Marwick. Because the development of the self-assessment was funded by the federal government, it is in the public domain.

Appendix 2

Books on Empowerment

Belasco, James, A. *Teaching the Elephant to Dance: Empowering Change in Your Organization*. New York: Crown Publishers, Inc., 1990.

Blanchard, Ken, Carlos, John P. and Randolph, Alan. *Empowerment Takes More Than a Minute*. San Francisco, CA: Berrett-Koehler, 1996.

Block, Peter. *The Empowered Manager: Positive Political Skills at Work*. San Francisco: Jossey-Bass Publishers, 1989.

Buchholz, Steve and Roth, Thomas. *Creating the High Performance Work Team*. New York: John Wiley & Sons, 1987.

Byham, Willam C., Ph.D. and Cox, Jeff. Heroz: *Empower Yourself, Your Coworkers, Your Company*. New York, NY: Harmony Books, 1994.

Byham, William C., Ph.D. *Zapp! Empowerment in Health Care: How to Improve the Quality of Patient Care, Increase Job Satisfaction and Lower Health Care Costs*. New York, NY: Fawcett Books, 1993.

Byham, William C., Ph.D. with Cox, Jeff. *Zapp! The Lightning of Empowerment*. New York, NY: Harmony, 1988.

Carlzon, Jan. *Moments of Truth*. Cambridge, MA: Ballinger Publishing Company, 1987.

Carr, Clay. *Teampower: Lessons from America's Top Companies on Putting Teamwork to Work*. Englewood Cliffs, NJ: Prentice-Hall, 1992.

Chang, Richard Y. and Curtin, Mark J. *Succeeding as a Self-Managed Team*. Irvine, CA: Richard Chang Associates, Inc., 1994.

Clemmer, Jack. *Firing on All Cylinders: The Service/Quality System for High-Powered Corporate Performance*. Toronto, ON, Canada: MacMillan, 1990.

Covey, Stephen. *Principle-Centered Leadership*. New York: Summit Books 1991.

Covey, Stephen. *The 7 Habits of Highly Effective People*. New York, NY: Simon & Schuster, 1989.

DePree, Max. *Leadership is an Art*. New York: Dell, 1989.

Fisher, Kimball. *Leading Self-Directed Work Teams: A Guide to Developing New Team Leadership Skills*. New York, NY: McGraw Hill, Inc., 1993.

Frangos, Stephen J. and Bennett, Steven J. *Team Zebra: How 1,500 Partners Revitalized Eastman Kodak's Black & White Film-Making Flow*. Essex Junction, VT: Omneo, 1993.

Hall, Jay. *The Competence Connection: A Blueprint for Excellence*. Woodlands, TX: Woodstead Press, 1988.

Hanna, David P. *Designing Organizations for High Performance.* Reading, MA: Addison-Wesley, 1988.

Harvey, Jerry. *The Abilene Paradox and Other Meditations on Management.* Lexington, MA: Lexington Books, 1988.

Hesselbein, Frances; Goldsmith, Marshall; Beckhard, Richard; Editors, *The Drucker Foundation. Leader of the Future.* San Francisco, CA: Jossey-Bass Publishers, 1996.

Kelly, Mark. *The Adventures of a Self-Managed Team.* San Diego: Pfeiffer & Co., 1991.

Kinlaw, Dennis. *Developing Superior Work Teams: Building Quality and the Competitive Edge.* San Diego, CA: University Associates, 1991.

Kouzes, Jim and Posner, Barry. *The Leadership Challenge: How to Get Extraordinary Things Done in Organizations.* San Francisco, CA: Jossey-Bass Publishers, 1987.

Lareu, William. *American Samurai.* Clinton NJ: New Win Publications, 1991.

Lawler, Edward E. III; Mohrman, Susan A. and Ledford, Gerald E. *Creating High Performance Organizations: Survey of Practices and Results of Employee Involvement and TQM in Fortune 1000 Companies.* San Francisco: Jossey-Bass Publishers, 1995.

Lawler, Edward E. III; Ledford, Gerald E. Jr; and Mohrman, Susan Albers. *Employee Involvement in America: A Study of Contemporary Practice.* Houston, TX: American Productivity & Quality Center, 1989.

Lawler, Edward E. III; Mohrman, Susan Albers; and Ledford, Gerald E. *Employee Involvement and Total Quality Management: Practices and Results in Fortune 1000 Companies.* San Francisco, CA: Jossey-Bass Publishers, 1992.

Lawler, Edward E. III. *High-Involvement Management.* San Francisco, CA: Jossey-Bass, Publishers, 1986.

Lawler, Edward E. III, Mohrman, Susan Albers and Ledford, Gerald E. *The Ultimate Advantage: Creating the High Involvement Organization.* San Francisco, CA: Jossey-Bass Publishers, 1992.

Lipnack, Jessica P. and Stamps, Jeffrey S. *The Team Net Factor: Bringing the Power of Boundary-Crossing Into the Heart of Your Business.* Essex Junction, VT: Oliver Wight Publications, Inc., 1993.

Manz, Charles C. and Sims, Henry P., Jr. *Business Without Bosses: How Self-Managing Teams are Building High-Performing Companies.* New York, NY: John Wiley & Sons, 1993.

McNally, David. *Even Eagles Need a Push.* Eden Prairie, MN: Transform Press, 1990.

Melohn, Tom. *The New Partnership: Profit By Bringing Out the Best in Your People, Customers and Yourself.* Essex Junction, VT: Omneo, 1994.

Mills, Daniel Quinn. *The Empowerment Imperative: Six Steps to a High Performance Organization.* Amhurst, MA: Human Resources Development Press, 1994.

Mohrman, Susan A., Cohen, Susan G. and Mohrman, Allan M. *Designing Team-*

Based Organizations: New Forms for Knowledge Work. San Francisco, CA: Jossey-Bass Publishers, 1995.

Mohrman, S. A. and Cummings, T. G. *Self-Designing Organizations: Learning How to Create High Performance.* Reading, PA: Addison-Wesley, 1989.

Orsburn, Jack D., Moran, Linda, Musselwhite, Ed, Zenger, John H. *Self-Directed Work Teams.* Homewood, IL: Business One Irwin, 1990.

Parker, Glenn M. *Team Players and Teamwork: The New Competitive Business Strategy.* San Francisco, CA: Jossey-Bass Publishers, 1990.

Parry, Scott B. *From Managing to Empowering: An Action Guide to Developing Winning Facilitation Skills.* White Plains, NY: Quality Resources, 1994.

Rancourt, Karen. *The Empowered Professional: How to Succeed in the 90's.* Harvard, MA: James Rue Books, 1990.

Richey, David L. and Richey, Fred W. *Empowerment: How to Stay a Knight.* Ventura, CA: Quality Groups Publishing, 1993.

Scott, Cynthia D., Ph.D. and Jaffe, Dennis, Ph.D. *Empowerment: Building a Committed Organization.* Los Altos, CA: Crisp Publications, Inc., 1991.

Semler, Ricardo. *Maverick: The Success Story Behind the World's Most Unusual Workplace.* New York, NY: Warner Books, 1993.

Shonk, James. *Team-Based Organizations: Developing a Successful Team Environment.* Homewood, IL: Business One Irwin, 1992.

Torres, Cresencio and Spiegal, Jerry. *Self-Directed Work Teams: A Primer.* San Diego, CA: Pfeiffer, 1990.

Truell, George F. *Employee Involvement: A Guidebook for Managers.* Buffalo, NY: PAT Publications, 1991.

Vogt, Judith F. and Murrell, Kenneth L. *Empowerment in Organizations.* San Diego, CA: University Associates, Inc., 1990.

Weisbord, Marvin R. *Discovering Common Ground: How Future Search Conferences Bring People Together to Achieve Breakthrough Innovation, Empowerment, Shared Vision and Collaborative Action.* San Francisco, CA: Berrett-Koehler Publishers, Inc., 1992.

Wellins, Richard S., Byham, William C., and Wilson, Jeanne M. *Empowered Teams: Creating Self-Directed Work Groups That Improve Quality, Productivity and Participation.* San Francisco, CA: Jossey-Bass, Publishers, 1991.

Wellins, Richard S., Byham, William C. and Dixon, George R. *Inside Teams: How 20 World-Class Organizations are Winning Through Teamwork.* San Francisco, CA: Jossey-Bass Publishers, 1994.

Wilson, Jeanne M., George, Jill, and Wellins, Richard S., with Byham, William C. *Leadership Trapeze: Strategies for Leadership in Team-Based Organizations.* San Francisco, CA: Jossey-Bass Publishers, 1994.

Zenger, John H., Musselwhite, Ed, Hurson, Kathleen and Perrin, Craig. *Leading Teams: Mastering the New Role.* Burr Ridge, IL: Irwin, 1994.

Index

AAL, Aid Association for Lutherans, 4, 26, 231-241
Abdicate, abdicating, anarchy 16, 34, 45, 94
Accountability, 21, 24, 40, 55, 62, 174, 176, 183, 184, 187, 213-217, 245, 249, 251
Allstate, 4, 135-147
American Productivity & Quality Center (APQC), 69, 72, 77
Appraisal (see performance)
Assessment, analysis, 56, 57, 66, 73-77, 96, 112, 125, 222, 237, 249
AT&T
   Microelectronics, 4, 201-211
   Universal Card Services, 64, 70
Authority, 26, 35, 36, 38, 39, 40, 71, 73
Autonomy, autonomous, 16, 71, 104, 108, 196
Awards (see recognition)

Barriers, 12, 86, 97, 115, 128, 145, 206, 236
Behaviors (see empowerment)
Beliefs (see values)
Benchmarking, 53, 54, 74, 82, 109, 160, 188
Bonus (see rewards)
Boundaries (see empowerment)
BP America, 29

Celebration (also see recognition), 13, 67, 117, 182, 189, 197, 240, 248
Center for Effective Organizations, 23, 72
Change, (also see transformation), 3, 11, 24, 63, 64, 66, 73, 87, 88, 93, 100, 111, 123, 125, 126, 128, 132, 133, 136, 138, 139, 142, 146, 180, 182, 199, 218-230, 232, 233, 239, 243

Chrysler, 4, 6, 190-200
Club Med, 74
Coaching, coaches, 13, 26, 30, 45, 47-48, 66, 67, 87, 108, 129, 130, 143, 146, 157, 228, 237, 247, 252
Colgate-Palmolive, 26
Command-and-control, 3, 32-41, 126, 130, 134, 135, 180, 223-224
Commitment, 6, 12, 28, 39, 48, 98, 119, 145, 183
Communication, communicating, 11, 12, 20, 27, 36, 40, 42, 44, 47, 49, 67, 68, 98, 102-112, 131-132, 138, 140, 143, 145, 175, 178, 181, 187, 214, 222, 227, 234, 240, 245, 249
Compensation (see rewards)
Conflict resolution, 57, 95, 214, 228, 229
Continuous improvement, (also see improvement and quality), 24, 92, 146, 167, 191, 214, 215, 216, 218, 235, 245, 247, 252, 253, 254
Control, controls, 18, 21, 28, 35, 36-39, 41, 42, 46, 47, 55, 63, 154, 156, 186
Corning, 192
Costs, 72, 73, 123, 194, 195, 215, 216, 227
Cross-functional teams (see teams)
Culture, 35, 41, 66, 76, 87, 105, 197, 207, 219, 232, 247, 254
Customer
   needs, requirements, expectations, 4, 11, 45, 72, 76, 170, 214, 240
   satisfaction, 82, 99, 100, 103, 108, 131, 158, 160, 214, 216, 233, 237, 239, 242, 244
   service, 31, 46, 48, 73, 88
   visits, relationships, 74, 121, 122, 161
Cycle time (also see process and turnaround time), 123, 158-167, 183, 227

Decisions, decision making, 25, 28, 39, 52, 55, 56, 71, 72, 73, 86, 88, 92, 94, 99, 114, 118, 120, 126, 137, 155, 183, 184, 186, 206, 213, 252
Delegate, delegation, 28, 34
Development Dimensions International (DDI), 26, 28
Discretion, discretionary effort, 71, 140
Disempowerment, 18, 19, 36, 41, 42
Diversity, 127, 144, 146

Empowerment
behaviors, 10, 12, 13, 16, 18, 19, 21, 34, 36, 41, 42, 44-51, 55, 67, 141, 145, 225, 229
boundaries, 12, 32-42, 45, 49, 56, 79, 83-87, 89, 94, 188, 213-217, 237, 238, 249
characteristics, 24-31
definition, 3, 17, 24-25, 33-34
let go, 7, 114, 115, 140, 166
pitfalls, 41-42
principles, 2, 11-13, 29, 246
roles (also see responsible), 9-10, 12, 22, 30, 32, 35, 44-50, 54, 55, 92, 93, 94, 199, 214, 215, 220, 229, 237, 238
understanding, 14-77

Facilitate, facilitator, facilitation, 13, 46, 90, 108, 127, 130, 143, 169, 186, 188, 191, 196, 219, 221, 223, 225, 228, 252
Federal Express, 4, 70, 74, 102-112
Feedback (see performance)
Frisch's Restaurants, 28

Gainsharing (see rewards)
General Electric, 25, 182
General Foods, 29
General Motors, 29
Goals and objectives, 17, 18, 21, 26, 44, 46, 47, 49, 55, 67, 92, 95, 105, 106, 118, 196, 201, 229, 240, 250
Golomski, Bill, 239

Hannaford Brothers Company, 30
Harris
  Corporation, 29, 64
  Semiconductor, 4, 218-230
Hierarchy/hierarchical, 126-127, 137, 205
Hewlett-Packard, 25
Hiring, selection, 27, 28, 67, 76, 128, 198, 249, 250

IBM, 25
Implementation Partners, 183
Improving, improvement (also see continuous improvement and quality) 7, 21, 48, 63, 96-97, 120, 125, 191, 195, 199
Information, 12, 15, 21, 22, 40, 46, 47, 55, 58, 65, 71, 107, 110, 112, 114, 115, 123, 132, 134, 144, 145, 203, 222, 225, 226, 237, 240
Investment, 100, 103, 144, 235, 246
Involvement, 3, 4, 15, 40, 42, 70-77, 92, 146, 182, 199, 206, 222-223

Johnsonville Foods, 27
Juran Institute, 239

Knowledge worker, 139-141

Lake Superior Paper Industries, 27
Leaders, leadership, leading, 8-9, 28, 44-46, 111, 141, 142, 145, 183, 185, 187, 199, 230, 235, 243, 249, 251-252
Lead-Empower-Assess-Partner (LEAP), 8-9
Let go (see empowerment)
Litton Guidance and Control Systems, 29
Lucent Technologies, 211
L.L. Bean, 74

3M, 64
Malcolm Baldrige National Quality Award, 61, 102, 106, 109, 239
Marriott, 4, 6, 70, 74, 79-89
Martin Marietta, 4, 90-101
Measures, measurement, metrics, indicators, 24, 26, 40, 47, 55, 56, 58,

66, 83, 95, 99, 106, 108, 112, 117, 139, 177, 188, 199, 225, 233-235, 237, 238, 241
Miller, Larry, 220
Miller Brewing Company, 30
Mind-set, 7-9, 17, 252
Mission, 55, 92, 93, 95
Monsanto, 4, 124-134
Motorola, 4, 158-167, 192

Nordstrom, 74

Organizational design, 20-22, 35, 125, 126, 134, 174, 220
Ownership, buy-in, 30, 45, 48, 62, 66, 145, 206, 207, 227

Pacific Gas & Electric, 4, 6, 179-189
Participative management, 3, 34, 47, 48, 52, 202, 206
Pay (see rewards)
Performance
    appraisal, evaluation, review, 22, 30, 40, 67, 99, 112, 130, 131, 237-238, 250
    expectations, 26, 29
    feedback, 35, 46, 49, 110
    general, 7, 11, 16, 21, 28, 55, 72, 235-237, 242
    360-degree feedback, 237-238
Plan-Organize-Direct-Control, 7-8
Power, 5, 7, 15, 16, 19, 20, 22, 34, 54, 118, 122, 240
Principles (see empowerment)
Problem solving, 20, 48, 49, 52, 64, 66, 71, 80, 108, 110, 118, 183, 191, 204, 206, 218
Process, processes, (also see cycle time and turnaround time), 48, 187, 194, 198, 199, 223, 224, 239
Procter & Gamble, 29
Productivity, 4, 11, 24, 25, 30, 31, 72, 99, 125-126, 128-130, 190, 191, 192, 194, 195, 198, 232, 233, 234, 237, 239
Profit sharing (see rewards)
Psychological, 17-19, 22, 27

Quality (also see improvement and continuous improvement), 4, 11, 24, 25, 31, 58, 59, 72, 79, 81, 108, 109, 117, 123, 125, 145, 158, 176, 177, 178, 191, 192, 197, 205, 206, 213, 227, 238, 244, 252
Quality circles, 3, 4, 15, 28, 71, 191, 197
Quality & Productivity Management Association (QPMA), 2, 72

Recognize, recognition (also see celebration), 13, 17, 24, 27, 40, 41, 45, 46, 47, 63, 67, 71, 73, 105-106, 125, 146, 182, 197, 225, 240, 242, 253
Rensis Likert, 202
Resist, resistance, 6, 66, 73, 93, 175, 177, 185, 221
Responsible, responsibility (also see empowerment roles), 5, 24, 26, 28, 30, 33, 35, 45, 65, 88, 92, 94, 97, 129, 140, 183, 196, 214, 215, 217, 223, 225, 229, 245, 249, 252
Results, outcomes, benefits, 5, 6, 7, 10, 21, 22, 24, 44, 46, 68, 136, 179, 188, 190, 193, 196, 197, 207-209, 236-237, 240, 242-243, 246, 248, 251
Review (see performance)
Rewards
    bonus, 67, 105-106, 236, 242, 248, 249-250
    compensation, 27, 73, 235-237, 250
    gainsharing, 72, 125, 127, 134, 136 237
    general, 15, 17, 27, 39, 41, 46, 47 63, 67, 71, 72-73, 125
    incentives, 116
    pay, 22, 67, 106, 128, 241
    pay-for-knowledge, 236
    pay-for-performance, 72
    pay-for-skills, 247, 250
Risks, risk taking, 46, 48, 62, 83, 115, 134
Rockwell International, 29
Roles (see empowerment)

Salaried workforce, 127, 247, 250
Saturn, 4, 64, 74, 213-217
Scandinavian Airlines, 70, 74
Self-directed work teams (see teams)
Shingo Prize, 201, 208, 242
Sociological, 19-20
Strategy, strategic plan, 16, 17, 21, 26, 44, 45, 49, 59, 61-68, 70-77, 117, 150, 229, 246
Suggestion systems, 28
Supervisors, supervision, 28, 30, 47-48, 51-59, 72, 104, 223, 226, 248
Surveys
  customer, 165, 170, 177, 182,
  employee, 92, 106, 109-110, 143, 145, 181, 207, 234
Swedish American Hospital, 4, 6, 168-178

Team building, 54, 99, 204, 225
Teams
  action, 80-81, 85, 179-189
  ad hoc, 2, 5
  business, 126
  cross-functional, 90, 117, 160, 165, 166, 169, 178, 181, 184, 201, 203
  general, 4, 16, 26, 29, 30, 120, 137, 143, 145, 157, 166, 169, 192, 197, 201-211, 241
  natural work groups, 202, 203, 205
  product development, 120, 121
  project, 71, 248, 250-251
  self-directed, self-managed 4, 5, 8, 27, 30, 71, 80, 89, 90, 91, 96, 97, 100, 120 123, 125, 139, 143, 213-253
  slice, 248, 250-251
Technology, 24, 74, 76, 110, 138, 140, 142, 143, 145, 149- 157, 234
Tennalum, 4, 242-253
Texas Instruments, 29, 64
Total quality management, TQM, 4, 8, 61, 79, 89, 168, 169, 178
Traditional, 3, 41, 72, 79-80, 97, 105, 201, 220, 224, 241, 246, 249, 253
Training, education, 12, 28, 29, 30, 33, 46, 47, 51-59, 66, 67, 71, 73, 79, 81-83, 86, 87, 90-100, 109, 112, 115, 128, 132, 134, 137, 138, 140, 146, 154, 155, 161, 169, 191, 193, 194, 195, 196, 197-199, 204, 207, 221, 223, 225-228, 230, 249, 252
Trane Co., 26
Transformation (also see change), 53, 125, 136-141, 146, 231, 232, 233, 235
Trust, 6, 12, 39, 93, 97, 115, 116, 130, 143, 146, 155, 221, 223, 225, 247, 251
Turnaround time (also see cycle time and process), 168-178

Unions, 10, 11, 15, 49-50, 133, 185, 186, 189, 191, 192, 193, 194, 203
Unisys Corporation, 29
USAA, 4, 6, 74, 149-157
U.S. General Accounting Office, 72

Values, beliefs, 5, 6, 11, 12, 24, 25, 27, 47, 92, 123, 134, 192, 246,
Vision, direction, 24, 25, 27, 34, 42, 44, 47, 49, 65, 66, 81, 87, 88, 93, 133, 137, 142, 145, 229, 237, 242-253

Xerox, 192

Zytec, 4, 113-123